"'Call the Sabbath a delight,' bids the Lor[d] ... Waters helps us to do just that. Tracing t[he] ... commands for keeping the Sabbath day ho[ly] ... nize this often-misunderstood day as essential for our growth in grace. Thanks to Waters's accessible writing and thorough exegesis, this book leaves readers with a clear sense of what the Lord commands and a fresh conviction that 'his commandments are not burdensome' (1 John 5:3). In a day when Christians talk frequently about the practice of 'Sabbath,' Waters invites us to see that the biblical Sabbath is much more than a day to enjoy bodily rest—it's a day to enjoy God himself."

Megan Hill, author, *Praying Together* and *A Place to Belong*; Managing Editor, The Gospel Coalition

"How and whether we are to observe the Sabbath commandment today has proven to be a tricky question. Waters helps us navigate this complexity with nuanced simplicity. He explains the role of Sabbath in creation and redemption, covering key texts from the Old and New Testaments. He covers tricky issues, like the way Jesus related to the Sabbath and why the Sabbath is now celebrated on Sunday. Waters also shows the ongoing relevance of the Sabbath and provides practical suggestions for observing the Sabbath today. This short book is long on helpful insights: it will show you why the Sabbath is good news, how it relates to Jesus himself, and why it is important that we continue to observe it today."

Brandon D. Crowe, Professor of New Testament, Westminster Theological Seminary

"What a timely and necessary book, calling us out of our fast-paced and productivity-driven lives to rightly regard and observe the Sabbath. Waters expertly moves us from Genesis to Revelation, tracing the Sabbath through creation, redemption, and consummation. Far from an outdated practice, the Sabbath day is a necessary reset that gives us perspective and promotes fruitfulness during our six days of labor. Waters reminds us that the Sabbath rest is an important means of imitating God and a weekly invitation to enjoy him. I found myself longing for the Sabbath, ready to joyfully submit to this command given at the beginning of time."

Colleen D. Searcy, Bible teacher; speaker; creator, Meet Me in the Bible resources

The Sabbath as Rest and Hope for the People of God

Short Studies in Biblical Theology

Edited by Dane C. Ortlund and Miles V. Van Pelt

The Sabbath as Rest and Hope for the People of God

Guy Prentiss Waters

WHEATON, ILLINOIS

The Sabbath as Rest and Hope for the People of God

Copyright © 2022 by Guy Prentiss Waters

Published by Crossway
        1300 Crescent Street
        Wheaton, Illinois 60187

Cover illustration and design: Jordan Singer

First printing 2022

Printed in the United States of America

Paperback ISBN: 978-1-4335-7354-5
ePub ISBN: 978-1-4335-7357-6
PDF ISBN: 978-1-4335-7355-2
Mobipocket ISBN: 978-1-4335-7356-9

Library of Congress Cataloging-in-Publication Data

Names: Waters, Guy Prentiss, 1975- author.
Title: The Sabbath as rest and hope for the people of God / Guy Prentiss Waters.
Description: Wheaton, Illinois : Crossway, 2022. | Series: Short studies in biblical theology | Includes bibliographical references and index.
Identifiers: LCCN 2022001337 (print) | LCCN 2022001338 (ebook) | ISBN 9781433573545 (paperback) | ISBN 9781433573576 (epub) | ISBN 9781433573569 (mobipocket) | ISBN 9781433573552 (pdf)
Subjects: LCSH: Sabbath. | Sunday. | Rest–Religious aspects–Christianity.
Classification: LCC BV111.3 .W38 2022 (print) | LCC BV111.3 (ebook) | DDC 263/.3–dc23/eng/20220224
LC record available at https://lccn.loc.gov/2022001337
LC ebook record available at https://lccn.loc.gov/2022001338

Crossway is a publishing ministry of Good News Publishers.

BP			30	29	28	27	26	25	24	23	22
14	13	12	11	10	9	8	7	6	5	4	3	2	1

Contents

Series Preface

Most of us tend to approach the Bible early on in our Christian lives as a vast, cavernous, and largely impenetrable book. We read the text piecemeal, finding golden nuggets of inspiration here and there, but remain unable to plug any given text meaningfully into the overarching storyline. Yet one of the great advances in evangelical biblical scholarship over the past few generations has been the recovery of biblical theology—that is, a renewed appreciation for the Bible as a theologically unified, historically rooted, progressively unfolding, and ultimately Christ-centered narrative of God's covenantal work in our world to redeem sinful humanity.

This renaissance of biblical theology is a blessing, yet little of it has been made available to the general Christian population. The purpose of Short Studies in Biblical Theology is to connect the resurgence of biblical theology at the academic level with everyday believers. Each volume is written by a capable scholar or churchman who is consciously writing in a way that requires no prerequisite theological training of the reader. Instead, any thoughtful Christian disciple can track with and benefit from these books.

Each volume in this series takes a whole-Bible theme and traces it through Scripture. In this way readers not only learn about a given theme but also are given a model for how to read the Bible as a coherent whole.

We have launched this series because we love the Bible, we love the church, and we long for the renewal of biblical theology in the academy to enliven the hearts and minds of Christ's disciples all around the world. As editors, we have found few discoveries more thrilling in life than that of seeing the whole Bible as a unified story of God's gracious acts of redemption, and indeed of seeing the whole Bible as ultimately about Jesus, as he himself testified (Luke 24:27; John 5:39).

The ultimate goal of Short Studies in Biblical Theology is to magnify the Savior and to build up his church—magnifying the Savior through showing how the whole Bible points to him and his gracious rescue of helpless sinners; and building up the church by strengthening believers in their grasp of these life-giving truths.

Dane C. Ortlund and Miles V. Van Pelt

Introduction

Over the last several decades, the Sabbath has undergone rapid decline in American life. A Sabbathless world promises heightened productivity and greater economic gain. It flatters the illusion that we have autonomous control over our schedules and our lives. But it leaves its frenetic inhabitants weary and empty. We deprive ourselves of the very thing that we most need—rest.

This book is not a plea to state and federal legislators to put blue laws back on the books. It is, rather, an exploration of what the Bible says to all human beings about the Sabbath. Many associate the Sabbath with Judaism or with certain movements in Protestant Christianity (e.g., Puritanism), but the Scripture teaches that the Sabbath concerns every human being. God has given us one day every week to remind us of some of the most important truths about himself, the world, and ourselves—he created us to worship him and to enjoy fellowship with him; he has redeemed sinners at the cost of his own Son, Jesus Christ; he has prepared a heavenly rest for each and every one of his people. In our 24/7 world, it is easy to lose sight of these basic truths. The Sabbath offers all people a weekly reset. In taking up God's call to meet with him in Jesus Christ on his appointed day, we find renewed clarity of vision. We see God, the world, and ourselves for what they really are. More than that, we find rest and refreshment of soul and body. That renewal equips us to serve God faithfully for the rest of the week, and it points us toward our heavenly home that lies at the end of our earthly pilgrimage.

In this book, we are undertaking a biblical theology of the Sabbath.[1] The Sabbath appears in Genesis, in Revelation, and at many points in between. It is woven into the warp and woof of Scripture. Thus, we will look at the Bible's testimony to the Sabbath from cover to cover. In chapter 1, we will explore what God says about the Sabbath at the creation of the world. God built the Sabbath into the creation such that human beings have never been without the Sabbath. This weekly rest points to the glorious goal of human existence—that we would glorify God in drawing near to him in worship and adoration. We will also see that God instituted a covenant in the garden of Eden so that Adam (representing all human beings who would trace their ordinary descent from him) might bring himself and us into the everlasting rest to which that weekly rest pointed. Adam would have achieved that goal had he continued to be obedient to God. Sadly, he sinned and fell (and we sinned and fell in him). In mercy, God appointed a Savior, the last Adam, to do what Adam failed to do (by obeying God perfectly) and to undo what Adam did (by bearing on the cross the penalty for his people's sins). In this way, God brings sinners from every tribe, tongue, people, and race into that promised heavenly rest.

God set to work saving sinners right away, and thus he began to prepare the world for the arrival of Jesus Christ. In chapters 2 and 3, we will explore how the Law and the Prophets spoke of the Sabbath in such a way as to point the faith of God's people forward to their coming Savior. While retaining its significance as a creation

---

1. For a sketch of the project of biblical theology, see my book, *The Lord's Supper as the Sign and Meal of the New Covenant*, Short Studies in Biblical Theology (Wheaton, IL: Crossway, 2019), 15–16.

ordinance, the Sabbath comes to take on additional meaning as a redemptive commemoration of the exodus. Every week, Israel would remember that God had redeemed them from bondage in Egypt—a glimpse of the coming redemption that Christ would accomplish at the cross. The Prophets, in particular, remind us that God intends the Sabbath to be a day of joy and delight for all kinds of people as the redeemed gather in the presence of their Creator and Deliverer.

In the New Testament, Jesus Christ's teachings and miracles also had a lot to say about the Sabbath. In chapter 4, we will see how his earthly ministry served to clarify the Sabbath's true meaning and purpose. His miracles were glimpses into the restoration and redemption that he had come to bring sinners. And his teaching about the Sabbath both stripped away the burdens that human teachers had laid upon it as well as highlighted the genuine joy and freedom that sinners receive and experience through faith in him.

But it was the resurrection of Christ from the dead that transformed the Sabbath. In chapter 5, we will see how the Gospels, Acts, the Letters, and Revelation all point to "the first day of the week" as the day on which the new covenant community, by divine commandment, gathers to worship God. As the seventh day of the week commemorated God's work of creation, so the first day of the week commemorates God's work of new creation, which dawned in human history at Christ's resurrection. As such, it comes to be known as "the Lord's day" (Rev. 1:10)—Christ's name is stamped upon this day, a fitting tribute to the one on whom creation, redemption, and consummation converge.

Overall, a biblical theology of the Sabbath has a lot to say about how Christians and the church should observe the Sabbath today. Thus, in chapter 6, we will explore some of these practical implications. They speak to our mindset, our attitudes, our choices, and our relationships with other Christians. Honoring the Sabbath, we will see, is critical to the pursuit of a Christian life that is healthy and vibrant.

For many in the church, the Sabbath is little more than a point of contention, a list of dos and don'ts. For others, it is utterly foreign. If your impressions of the Sabbath are either negative or nonexistent, I hope that you'll come away from this book with a sense of the good that God intends in your life and mine when we take up his call to observe the Sabbath. After all, the Sabbath is a weekly invitation from God to draw close and enter into renewed fellowship with the one who made us and who redeemed sinners at the cost of his own Son. And it is a weekly reminder that in Christ, the best is yet to come. May this book encourage you to find and to experience the rest that you and I need in the only place where it can be found—Jesus Christ.

1

Creation

The Bible introduces the Sabbath at its beginning. We first meet the Sabbath in the account of God making heaven and earth (Gen. 1:1–2:3). Strikingly, it is *God* who, in a sense, observes the first Sabbath (2:3). In this chapter, we are going to look, with the help of the New Testament, at what Genesis says about that Sabbath. We will make the case that God intends all human beings to observe a weekly Sabbath as a day of holy resting. We will then see that the Sabbath is a window into what God intended for the world at its creation. In this respect, the Sabbath is eschatological—that is to say, it points to the goal that God had for creation from the very beginning. Although the fall of humanity into sin appeared to thwart that goal, our fall in Adam actually prepared the way for its fulfillment in the last Adam, Jesus Christ. The Sabbath, then, draws together the great concerns of the Bible—creation, redemption, and the glory of God in Jesus Christ.

God Works, God Rests

In the creation account, God makes the world and everything in it in six days. A seventh day follows that is set apart from the previous six in some important ways. Genesis 2:1–3 reads,

Thus the heavens and the earth were finished, and all the host of them. And on the seventh day God finished his work that he had done, and he rested on the seventh day from all his work that he had done. So God blessed the seventh day and made it holy, because on it God rested from all his work that he had done in creation.

These verses conclude the account of God's creating the world that started in Genesis 1:1.[1] We may now look at what they tell us about God and the creation and then further reflect on their message in light of Genesis 1:1–2:3 as a whole.

First, it is clear that the work of creation is completed—verse 1 reads, "the heavens and the earth were finished, and all the host of them" (cf. 1:2, 30). This work was done in six days, so the seventh day will be different. It is not a day of work for God, but rest—verses 2 and 3 say that he "rested on the seventh day from all his work that he had done" and that "on [the seventh day] God rested from all his work that he had done in creation." Though the word "Sabbath" does not appear here, a related word does. The Hebrew verb translated "rested" (*shbt*) in Genesis 2:2–3 is related to the Hebrew noun translated "Sabbath" (*shabbat*). There is, therefore, an implicit connection established between God's rest and what later revelation will call the "Sabbath."

Further, the beginning of Genesis shows us that this day is set apart from the previous six days in at least two more ways. In the first place, it is a day that "God blessed" (2:3). Earlier, God is said to have "blessed" the birds and the sea creatures and to have "blessed" Adam and Eve at their creation (1:22, 28). In each case that benediction is

---

1. The next verse begins with the phrase, "These are the generations." Commentators often point out that this clause serves as the marker of a new section within Genesis (see Gen. 5:1; 6:9; 10:1; 11:10; 11:27; 25:12; 25:19; 36:1; 36:9; 37:2). The first portion of the section that follows, Genesis 2:4–25, offers a more detailed account of the way in which God created the first humans, Adam and Eve, on the sixth day (cf. 1:26–31).

followed by the command to "be fruitful and multiply and fill" (1:22, 28). Thus, when God blesses the seventh day, our expectation is that this day will be marked by fruitfulness and fullness appropriate to that day.

In the second place, God "made [the seventh day] holy" (2:3). This is the first time in Genesis that God is said to make something "holy," and it means that this seventh day was deemed different from the other six days. What distinguishes the "holy" seventh day is that it is set apart for purposes of worship.[2]

The resting in view on this seventh day is therefore a holy resting. To be sure, it is a day marked by the cessation of God's work in creating the world and everything in it. But that cessation is only the penultimate characteristic of the day. The ultimate characteristic of the day is worship, a worship that is tied to fruitfulness and fullness.

THE SABBATH: GOD'S ORDINANCE FOR HUMAN BEINGS

This observation raises the question, "What kind of worship is in view, and by whom?" The answer of Genesis is, "Humanity's worship of the God who made them." Human beings are unique within Genesis 1:1–2:3 as those said to be made after the "image" and "likeness" of God (1:26), after God's "own image, in the image of God" (1:27). As such, people are uniquely capable among all the creatures mentioned in Genesis 1:1–2:3 of fellowship and communion with God.[3] Thus, the worship for which God provides in Genesis 2:1–3 is given so that his image bearers may have fellowship with him. Strikingly,

---

2. Gregory K. Beale, *A New Testament Biblical Theology: The Unfolding of the Old Testament in the New* (Grand Rapids: Baker, 2011), 778. As Beale notes, "the use of the Piel stem of the Hebrew word *qādaš* found in Gen. 2:3, which is used the most throughout the OT, almost always refers to setting apart humans or things for human cultic use. However, the only days said to be 'set apart' or 'holy' in the OT are Sabbaths and various festival days" (778).

3. L. Michael Morales, *Who Shall Ascend the Mountain of the Lord? A Biblical Theology of the Book of Leviticus*, New Studies in Biblical Theology 37 (Downers Grove, IL: InterVarsity Press, 2015), 46.

then, "humanity . . . is not the culmination of creation, but rather humanity in Sabbath day communion with God."[4]

Genesis 1:1–2:3, in fact, presents a twofold imitation of God on the part of his image bearers. First, God creates human beings to work (1:28–30). In part, people express the image of God as they labor in their various callings. The God who exercises dominion over the works of his hands calls humanity to "have dominion" over the earth and all the animals in it (1:26). The God who fills the world that he has made calls human beings to "be fruitful and multiply and fill the earth and subdue it" (1:28). Thus, humans will exercise dominion as they are faithful to marry and produce offspring (see 2:23–25). But it would be a mistake to say that Genesis 1:1–2:3 conceives no higher human imitation of God than labor. As human beings imitate God at work, so also are they to imitate God at rest. As God made the world and everything in it within the space of six days and rested on the seventh day, so are human beings to engage in six days of labor and one day of holy resting.

In sum, God intends for human beings to imitate his rest by taking the weekly Sabbath to rest from their labors and devote the whole day to his worship. The word translated "bless" (*barak*) in Genesis 2:3 "is normally restricted to living beings in the [Old Testament] and typically does not apply to something being blessed or sanctified only for God's sake."[5] Thus, God does not bless the seventh day for his own sake but for humanity's sake. He is setting apart this one day in seven to be a regular day of rest in the weekly cycle of human existence. He is, in effect, commanding human beings to observe the Sabbath. Further, we have noted above that the word translated "made . . . holy" (*qadas*) frequently relates to the worship of God in the Old Testament.[6] This clarifies that human beings are to observe

---

4. Morales, *Who Shall Ascend*, 47.

5. Beale, *New Testament Biblical Theology*, 778.

6. See footnote 2.

this seventh day as a day devoted to such worship. As it is dedicated
to the worship of God, the Sabbath promises blessing to human beings who comply with this divine command.

Exodus 20:8–11 confirms our findings from Genesis 2:1–3. Here,
God draws an explicit parallel between his creating the world in six
days but resting the seventh and human beings working six days but
resting the seventh. Exodus reads:

> Remember the Sabbath day, to keep it holy. Six days you shall
> labor, and do all your work, but the seventh day is a Sabbath
> to the LORD your God. . . . For in six days the LORD made
> heaven and earth, the sea, and all that is in them, and rested
> on the seventh day. Therefore the LORD blessed the Sabbath
> day and made it holy.

Thus the basis for the weekly Sabbath, according to Exodus, is
God's resting on the seventh day of Genesis 2:1–3.[7] This relationship between God's resting and the weekly Sabbath is precisely
what we have observed in Genesis itself, where this relationship
implicitly grounds the Sabbath command as a perpetual ordinance
for human beings.

In addition to this confirmation from Exodus, the New Testament provides indirect testimony to the Sabbath as an ordinance
for humanity established at the creation. Early in Mark's Gospel, we
read of a series of incidents in which Jesus comes under criticism
by the religious authorities (Mark 2:1–3:6). One of these incidents
takes place in "grainfields" through which Jesus and his disciples

---

7. John Murray observes that "even in Ex. 20:11 it is difficult to ascertain whether the sabbath day referred to is expressly the seventh day in the realm of God's activity or the seventh
day in man's weekly cycle." Even so, he continues, "the sabbath of God's rest is the reason given
for the sabbath of man's rest, the recurring seventh day of the week. And this would carry with
it the inevitable inference that God blessed and sanctified the seventh day of our week precisely
because he sanctified the seventh day in the realm of his own creative activity." John Murray,
Principles of Conduct (Grand Rapids, MI: Eerdmans, 1957), 31.

are traveling on the Sabbath (2:23). The Pharisees accuse Jesus of "doing what is not lawful on the Sabbath" (2:24). But he defends his disciples' activity as proper to the Sabbath day and then proceeds to clarify the true nature of the day. As he does so, he tells the Pharisees, "The Sabbath was made for man, not man for the Sabbath" (2:27). Here, Jesus makes at least three points that bear on our study of Genesis 2:1–3. The first is that the Sabbath is not unique to the Jew, nor is it exclusively intended for any other subset of the human race. Rather, it is something that pertains to human beings as human beings ("man").[8] The second point that Jesus makes is that the Sabbath "was made" for man. The passive voice here points to divine agency—it is God who made the Sabbath for human beings, and thus the Sabbath is a divine ordinance. Third, God instituted the Sabbath as a help to humanity ("for man"). The Sabbath is intended to promote and to further the purposes for which God made human beings. Although Jesus does not explain those purposes or how the Sabbath advances them in this passage, his words echo what we have observed from Genesis 1:1–2:3—that the Sabbath is a means to an end, specifically, the end for which God created human beings, which is to commune with him and to find rest and refreshment in this divine communion.

CONCLUSIONS

In conclusion, by setting aside the seventh day as a time of resting from his work of creating the world, God institutes the weekly Sabbath as an ongoing ordinance for human beings. The Sabbath commandment does not oblige Israel alone; it binds all human beings by virtue of them being made in the image of God. Thus, humanity did not receive the Sabbath commandment at some point far into the

---

8. Roger T. Beckwith and Wilfrid Stott, *This Is the Day: The Biblical Doctrine of the Christian Sunday in Its Jewish and Early Church Setting* (London: Marshall, Morgan & Scott, 1978), 11.

course of human history—God gave the Sabbath to humanity at the beginning of history, at the creation of the world.

So how are human beings to keep the Sabbath? And what does God intend to bring about through their Sabbath keeping? Humans are to imitate God by engaging in labor for six days of the week. But they are no less designed to imitate God by resting the seventh day. This means that God wants people, for twenty-four hours, to cease the work that occupies them six days of the week. Yet, that cessation of labor—and the refreshment that comes from that cessation—is a means to a greater end.[9] God wants human beings to worship him. The Sabbath is a day that God has "made . . . holy"—it is set apart to him and to his worship. And it is precisely because the day is directed toward God that it carries blessing for human beings. It is a day that God has "blessed." In light of the testimony of Genesis 1:1–2:3, that blessing carries potential for fruitfulness and fullness. Thus, as God meets with people who truly worship him on that day, they experience all of these gifts—spiritual blessing, fruitfulness, and fullness.

It is this latter point that brings us to the heart of the Sabbath. God made human beings to worship him, to have fellowship with him, and to find blessing and happiness in that worship and fellowship. We were created to labor, to be sure, but the ultimate goal of human existence is to worship and glorify the God who made us. As we read farther into Genesis 2, with the help of the New Testament, we get additional clarity and insight into how God disclosed that goal at the dawn of history. And that additional light will, in turn, help us to understand the beginnings of the Sabbath even better.

---

9. Geerhardus Vos rightly notes that the "rest" in view at Genesis 2:1–3 "stands for consummation of a work accomplished and the joy and satisfaction attendant upon this. Such was its prototype in God. Mankind must copy this." Geerhardus Vos, *Biblical Theology: Old and New Testaments* (Carlisle, PA: Banner of Truth, 1975), 140.

The Sabbath: Eschatological and Covenantal

When systematic theologians use the term "eschatological," they usually refer to the "four last things"—death, judgment, heaven, and hell. When biblical theologians use that term, they often have in mind a different but complementary definition. "Eschatology" brings into view the fact that human history has meaning and direction. Specifically, it has a *God-assigned* meaning and direction. History is going somewhere, namely, to the goal that God has set for it. This goal is one that he purposed in eternity and revealed at the very beginning of history—the blessed communion of image bearers with the God who made them (Gen. 1:1–2:3).

Genesis 2:4–25 helps us to understand that goal better. If Genesis 1 is the wide-angle portrait of God's creation of the world in six days, then Genesis 2 is the zoom-lens close-up of God's work on the sixth day. Here we learn that, after he had created Adam (2:7), God "planted a garden in Eden, in the east, and there he put the man whom he had formed" (2:8). God's purpose for setting Adam in the garden is that he would "work it and keep it" (2:15). He generously permits Adam to eat "of every tree of the garden" except for one, saying, "of the tree of the knowledge of good and evil you shall not eat, for in the day that you eat of it you shall surely die" (2:16–17).

Biblical theologians have termed this arrangement a "covenant." A covenant is an arrangement between two parties in an "existing" and "elective relationship."[10] In biblical covenants between God and human beings, this arrangement is initiated by God himself. In particular, God sovereignly administers promises with corresponding obligations. These covenants address life-and-death issues.[11]

---

10. The phrase "existing, elective relationship" is from Paul R. Williamson, *Sealed with An Oath: Covenant in God's Unfolding Purpose*, New Studies in Biblical Theology 23 (Downers Grove, IL: InterVarsity Press, 2007), 43.

11. I have drawn this definition in this paragraph from my book, *The Lord's Supper as the Sign and Meal of the New Covenant*, Short Studies in Biblical Theology (Wheaton, IL: Crossway,

Even though the word "covenant" does not appear in Genesis 2–3, we have the essence of a covenant in the garden.[12] By the time we arrive at the end of Genesis 2, we have learned that God and Adam are in an existing and elective relationship. Not only does God relate to Adam as the creature he has made (1:26–27), but God also chooses Adam, as a representative person, to undertake a project that will profoundly affect his descendants. Further, the arrangement that God imposes upon Adam is one of life-and-death issues, and its tragic outcome is death in all its fullness—physical and eternal. This arrangement, moreover, is sovereignly administered. God imposes these terms upon Adam. Adam receives them but sadly rejects them when he disobeys God's command, and death for him and his ordinary posterity is the consequence.[13]

The obligation of this covenant is clear enough—upon pain of death, Adam must not eat of the tree of the knowledge of good and evil (2:17). But where is the promise? What promise did God hold out to Adam? The promise is implicit in the command and the curse that accompanies it. When Adam disobeyed God, God justly passed the sentence of death upon him. But if Adam had obeyed God, he would have received life as the reward of his obedience. God implicitly promises life to Adam for obedience even as he explicitly threatens death for disobedience.

But this raises a further question. Adam was already alive when God made this promise to him. God made him righteous and holy (Eccles. 7:29), and he was already enjoying fellowship with God in the garden. How could God meaningfully offer life to someone who appeared to be enjoying life to the full? The answer to that question

---

2019), 21–26. The phrase "life and death" is from O. Palmer Robertson, *The Christ of the Covenants* (Phillipsburg, NJ: P&R, 1980), 4, 10.

12. Not all biblical theologians understand God to have entered into a covenant with Adam in the garden of Eden, in part because of the absence of the word "covenant" in Genesis 2.

13. The material in this paragraph has been drawn, with some adaptation, from my book, *The Lord's Supper*, 32.

arises from the sad fact of Adam's fall. When Adam sinned, he for-feited the life that he had in the garden. Once righteous, Adam was now guilty of sin and under the reign of sin. Once the friend of God, Adam now covered himself and hid himself from God (Gen. 3:7–8). All of this is to say that the life that Adam enjoyed in paradise was losable. Adam could—and did—forfeit the life of fellowship with God. So, we may say, what was promised to Adam in this first cove-nant (often called the covenant of works) was a secured or confirmed life.[14] We may also say, on the basis of what we will soon see from the testimony of the New Testament, that God was no less promising to Adam a heightened or intensified life. In other words, Adam would have enjoyed higher and greater degrees of the communion and fel-lowship with God than he was already enjoying in the garden.[15]

We are now in a position to draw together what we have seen both in Genesis 1 and 2. First, Genesis 1:1–2:3 shows us that human beings, God's image bearers, realize the goal of their existence in the worship and fellowship of their Creator. God's seventh-day resting from his labors of the six days of creation does not only *describe* the way in which God made the world. It also *prescribes* the way in which human beings are to order their lives—six days of labor and one day of holy resting. This day involves the setting down of the work of the six days in order to take up the work of the Sabbath day, namely, the worship of and communion with God.

Then, Genesis 2:4–25 reveals a covenant that God made with Adam that is designed to advance that goal of human existence. This covenant is marked by the generosity and kindness of God. God has set Adam in paradise and invites him to enjoy its bounty. He offers

---

14. Historically, theologians have termed this covenant the "covenant of works." The word "works" emphasizes the fact that the blessings offered to Adam in this covenant were suspended upon his obedience. In other words, Adam would secure the life of this covenant by his ongoing and perfect obedience to God.

15. The material from these last two sentences is drawn from my book *The Lord's Supper*, 32.

to Adam confirmed, heightened life in fellowship with him, provided that Adam refrain from eating the fruit of a single tree in the garden. This life, of course, is precisely the one that is envisioned in the seventh-day resting of Genesis 2:1–3. As Geerhardus Vos observes,

> The so-called "Covenant of Works" was nothing but an embodiment of the Sabbatical principle. Had its probation been successful, then the sacramental Sabbath would have passed over into the reality it typified, and the entire subsequent course of the history of the race would have been radically different. What now is to be expected at the end of this world would have formed the beginning of the world course instead.[16]

In other words, God's covenant with Adam in Genesis 2 was designed to advance humanity to its eschatological goal of Sabbath life with God.

Sadly, we may only think along these lines hypothetically. Adam fell into sin and, because Adam was our appointed representative (see Rom. 5:12–21), we sinned in him and fell with him in that first sin. From that point forward, death and not life would be the birthright of every human being ordinarily descended from Adam. Adam— and we in Adam—forfeited the Sabbath life that God had held out to him at the creation.

Thankfully, though, that is not the end of the human story. God sent his Son, the Lord Jesus Christ, to save sinners from death and to bring them to eschatological life. The saving work of Christ is the outworking of God's eternal plan to glorify himself through the redemption of sinners. This plan, Paul tells us in 1 Corinthians 15:42–49, encompasses the purposes for humanity that we have

---

16. Vos, *Biblical Theology*, 140.

seen God announce at the creation. In fact, Paul shows us here how creation and redemption, far from sitting uncomfortably next to one another, are part of an integrated whole. In particular, Paul shows us how the Sabbath goal for humanity, which was announced at the creation, comes to fulfillment in the person and work of the last Adam, Jesus Christ.

Jesus Christ, the Last Adam (1 Cor. 15:42–49)

In 1 Corinthians 15:1–58, Paul wants us to see the necessity and the nature of the bodily resurrection from the dead, and in the course of his argument, he compares our present bodies with our resurrection bodies in order to illustrate their differences (1 Cor. 15:42–44a).[17] His concluding observation in this series of comparisons is that "it is sown a natural body; it is raised a spiritual body" (15:44). This distinction (natural/spiritual) prompts the line of argumentation that follows in 15:44–49. Paul reasons, "If there is a natural body, there is also a spiritual body" (15:44). He grounds this claim in the following verse, "Thus it is written, 'The first man Adam became a living being'; the last Adam became a life-giving spirit" (15:45). Here, Paul quotes Genesis 2:7, the account of the creation of Adam. This quotation, and Paul's interpretation of and commentary on it, helps us to see clearly what Paul is comparing and contrasting. In sum, Paul sets before us two representative men: Adam ("the first man") and Christ ("the second man") (15:47). Their two bodies correspond to the two ages over which they preside and the "two different modes of existence pertaining to them."[18] Paul here is not principally comparing and contrasting the Adamic order as characterized by sin, corrup-

---

17. Some of the material that follows has been drawn from my work, "1-2 Corinthians," in Michael J. Kruger, ed., *A Biblical-Theological Introduction to the New Testament: The Gospel Realized* (Wheaton, IL: Crossway, 2016), 212–14.

18. Herman Ridderbos, *Paul: An Outline of His Theology*, trans. John R. DeWitt (Grand Rapids, MI: Eerdmans, 1975), 542.

tion, and death with the eschatological order inaugurated by Christ, the "last Adam." Rather, he is comparing and contrasting the Adamic order prior to the fall in its "original state" with the eschatological order that follows.[19] We know this because it is Adam-as-created (Gen. 2:7) that Paul mentions here.

Overall, Adam and Christ are similar to one another in that each is a representative man presiding over a distinct order of existence. Adam was created a "living being" (*psychēn zōsan*); Christ at his resurrection "became a life-giving spirit" (*pneuma zōopoioun*). Moreover, the words translated "being" and "spirit" in 1 Corinthians 15:45 are related to the words translated "natural" and "spiritual" in 15:44 and 15:46. However, Adam and Christ differ in that Adam became living (*zōsan*) at his creation but Christ became life-giving (*zōopoioun*) at his resurrection.[20] Adam, though created "living," fell into death through sin, plunging his ordinary posterity into death with him. Christ, on the other hand, conquered death in his death and resurrection (see 15:54–57); raised in the power of the Holy Spirit, possessed by and possessing the Spirit, he is now the "life-giving" last Adam. In sum, Adam forfeited life through his disobedience but Christ has secured life through his obedience, and this life he freely gives to his people by the Holy Spirit.

Paul is not simply saying that Christ follows Adam in time; nor is he saying that Christ has merely repaired what Adam damaged at the fall. He is claiming at 15:44 that one may infer the spiritual body from the natural body ("if there is a natural body, there is also a spiritual body"). This is so because "Adam, by virtue of creation (not because of sin), anticipates and points to another, higher form of [bodily] existence."[21] The covenant of works was designed to usher

---

19. Ridderbos, *Paul*, 542n152.

20. Richard B. Gaffin Jr., *Resurrection and Redemption: A Study in Paul's Soteriology*, 2nd ed. (Phillipsburg, NJ: P&R, 1987), 87–88.

21. Gaffin, *Resurrection and Redemption*, 82.

into human existence such fullness of eschatological life in communion with God. Adam failed to do this, choosing rather to sin against God. But the last Adam, by his obedience, death, and resurrection, has secured this eschatological life.[22] What creation was pointing toward, Jesus Christ has fulfilled and freely gives to his people through the ministry of the Holy Spirit.

Just like in the creation account, the word "Sabbath" is not found anywhere in 1 Corinthians 15:42–49. But the idea of the Sabbath pervades Paul's teaching in this passage for the simple reason that "the Sabbath is an expression of the eschatological principle on which the life of humanity has been constructed."[23] God instituted the weekly Sabbath at the creation in order to point to the goal of human existence, namely, eschatological life with God. That goal has been secured and realized in the redemptive work of Jesus Christ. And believers in Christ have already begun to share in that life by the Spirit, even as they will fully experience that life when their bodies are raised gloriously from the dead. Overall, this goal of human existence remains the same as it was at the creation of Adam. What has changed is that, in the last Adam, God has removed the barriers of sin and death and brought multitudes of human beings definitively and irreversibly into that life. Adam did not bring us there. We did not bring ourselves there. It is Christ who brings us there.

Our Sabbath Rest (Heb. 4)

One passage in the New Testament that speaks of the eschatological goal of humanity in terms of the Sabbath is Hebrews 3:7–4:13.

---

22. Christ has won redemption and life for sinners in every age of redemptive history as the covenant head of his people. The work of Christ was and is administered to human beings through what has been called the covenant of grace. This covenant is introduced in Genesis 3:15 and finds its climax in the new covenant, which began at the resurrection of Christ. The various covenants that God makes with human beings after the fall are administrations of this one covenant of grace. See further my book, *The Lord's Supper*, 33–41.

23. Vos, *Biblical Theology*, 140.

This section explicitly interprets the Sabbath rest of God in Genesis 2:1–3. Throughout this passage, the writer compares the church with Israel of the wilderness generation. Beginning with a citation of Psalm 95:7–11, the writer characterizes that generation as one that "rebelled," "sinned," was "disobedient," and was "unbelie[ving]" (Heb. 3:16, 17, 18, 19; cf. 4:6). He likewise warns the church against "an evil, unbelieving heart" and the "harden[ing]" of "the deceitfulness of sin" (3:12, 13). Notwithstanding the outward benefits that they received from God (3:9, 16), including "the good news" (4:6), the wilderness generation rebelled against God. Today, the church has "good news" offered to it just as it was offered to the wilderness generation (4:2) and must respond to God in faith, not by "the same sort of disobedience" (4:11) that made God "sw[ear] in [his] wrath, 'They shall not enter my rest'" (3:11, 18–19). In light of this divine oath, the writer warns the church, "While the promise of entering his rest still stands, let us fear lest any of you should seem to have failed to reach it" (4:1).

But what is this rest that the wilderness generation failed to attain and believers now are called to "enter" (4:1, 11)? The writer answers that question in 4:3–4:

For we who have believed enter that rest, as he has said,

"As I swore in my wrath,
'They shall not enter my rest,'"

although his works were finished from the foundation of the world. For he has somewhere spoken of the seventh day in this way: "And God rested on the seventh day from all his works."

In other words, the rest that lay before the wilderness generation, and that lies before the new covenant church, is the seventh-day rest of the creation (Gen. 2:1–3). God prevented the disobedient Israelites from entering into that rest. This point is confirmed by the writer's emphasis on the word "today" at the beginning of his citation of Psalm 95:7–11 (Heb. 4:7). This word, he argues, demonstrates that Joshua did not give Israel rest in the land, for if he had done so, "God would not have spoken of another day later on" (4:8)—that is to say, David would have not spoken in his own day (in Psalm 95) of a future rest if Joshua had already brought Israel into that rest.

Thus, this seventh-day creation rest is what the writer exhorts the church to enter (Heb. 4:11). He terms it "a Sabbath rest," saying, "so then, there remains a Sabbath rest [*sabbatismos*] for the people of God" (4:9). It is this rest that is entirely future to the believer (just as it was entirely future to our spiritual ancestors, Israel).[24] And it is this rest that will mark the conclusion of our wilderness sojourn as the people of God.

The writer does not in this section give an explicit command to Sabbath observance.[25] What he does, rather, is to say that the seventh-day rest of Genesis 2:1–3 is the rest that believers have yet to enter and that believers are called to enter. We will enter this rest in the way of faith in the "good news" (Heb. 4:6), a faith that does not let go of Christ (3:14), a faith that abounds in good works (see 4:10). Thus, this Sabbath rest is eschatological in that it is the goal of God for human beings and this rest is Christological in that we may only reach this goal through faith in the work of another, our "great high priest who has passed through the heavens, Jesus, the Son of God" (4:14).

These considerations speak to Sabbath observance even under the new covenant; God intends for his pattern of working six days

---

24. For a reply to the claim that Hebrews 4:3a and 4:10 demonstrate that this rest is presently enjoyed by the believer, see Richard B. Gaffin Jr., "A Sabbath Rest Still Awaits the People of God," eds., Charles Dennison and Richard Gamble, *Pressing Toward the Mark: Essays Commemorating Fifty Years of the Orthodox Presbyterian Church* (Philadelphia: The Committee for the Historian of the Orthodox Presbyterian Church, 1986), 41–46.

25. As Gaffin observes in "A Sabbath Rest," 41.

and resting the seventh to provide an abiding pattern for human beings (Gen. 2:1–3). The weekly Sabbath is a pointer and reminder of the purpose for which we were made as well as the goal to which God's people are moving—consummate, eschatological life in Jesus Christ. And the author to the Hebrews is telling us that this creational pattern continues with the arrival of the new covenant (Heb. 8:8–13). To be sure, Christ has "appeared once for all at the end of the ages" (9:26) "in these last days" (1:2). But we have not yet arrived at our "better country, that is, a heavenly one" (11:16), "the city that is to come" (13:14). Thus, the weekly Sabbath points us to our heavenly destination and calls us to "hold our original confidence firm to the end" (3:14).

Conclusions

Overall, the Sabbath is a microcosm of human history—creation, redemption, and consummation. It captures the purpose and goal of human existence (eschatological life with God) and acts as a perpetual reminder of that purpose and goal (Gen. 2:1–3). It comes to expression in the covenant of works (Gen. 2:15–17). After the fall of humanity into sin in Adam, God sends his beloved Son, the last Adam, to redeem his people. Christ does not merely repair what was destroyed or lost in Adam—he also advances his people to the goal for which they were created (1 Cor. 15:42–49). Thus, in Christ, we continue to observe the weekly Sabbath as a pointer toward our future rest and a help in our present pilgrimage (Heb. 4:9).

This is the rich biblical framework of the Sabbath, anchored in the creation itself. The Sabbath is a window into our own humanity and the kind of people that God calls us to be in Jesus Christ. In the chapters that follow we will trace the rich trajectory of the Sabbath across redemptive history, from the Law to the Prophets to Christ and his apostles.

2

Law

Although many people identify the Sabbath with Israel or Judaism, the Bible roots the Sabbath in the creation. It is a creation ordinance and thus valid for and binding on all people at all times and in all places. Even so, the Sabbath comes to take on special significance in the life of God's covenant people, Israel. The foundational biblical books that help us to see that significance are the first five books of the Bible, the Torah.

In this chapter, we are going to consider what the remainder of Genesis as well as Exodus through Deuteronomy have to say about the Sabbath. In these books, God builds upon the foundation that he has laid in creation. We will first look at one passage that helps us to see the place and observance of the Sabbath in the life of Israel prior to God's meeting with them at Mount Sinai. We will then look at what God says about the Sabbath in the Ten Commandments that he gave to Israel on Sinai; these commandments constitute the heart and center of the whole legislation that God would go on to give to his people in Exodus through Deuteronomy. Finally, we will look at some representative passages that help us to see the place and purpose of the Sabbath in that body of law.

From Eden to Sinai

Many have observed that the Sabbath does not emerge as a formal command in the Bible until God meets with Israel at Mount Sinai (Ex. 20). While that is true, we have seen that the Sabbath is implicitly commanded at creation. Furthermore, we have an account early in Israel's history of their observance of the Sabbath. This passage, Exodus 16:22–30, merits close observation.

At this point in the narrative, God has redeemed Israel from bondage to Egypt, miraculously delivering them through the Red Sea (14:1–31). Israel has responded in praise to the God who has "become [their] salvation" (15:2), who has "redeemed" the "people" whom "in [his] steadfast love" he is leading "to [his] holy abode" (15:13). And as they journey through the wilderness, God provides his people both water (15:22–27) and food (16:1–21), notwithstanding their grumbling (15:24; 16:2; cf. 16:7–9, 12).

When God provides this manna, he gives a bountiful portion for every Israelite (16:16–18). Moses commands them, furthermore, to gather manna daily and not "leave any of it over till the morning" (16:19). It is at that point that, "on the sixth day," Israel gathers "twice as much bread" as they ordinarily would have otherwise (16:22). An explanation for this comes in the following verse, which says, "This is what the LORD has commanded: 'Tomorrow is a day of solemn rest, a holy Sabbath to the LORD; bake what you will bake and boil what you will boil, and all that is left over lay aside to be kept till the morning" (16:23). In other words, God allows Israel to keep manna for the following day because on that day, the Sabbath, he will not provide manna "in the field" (16:25)—God proclaims, "Six days you shall gather it, but on the seventh day, which is a Sabbath, there will be none" (16:26).

Therefore, on the Sabbath day Israel must refrain from the daily task of gathering manna. God provides a double portion on the sixth day so that on the seventh day the Israelites may "remain each of [them] in his place" as no one is to "go out of his place on the seventh day" (16:29); it is a day on which the Israelites "rested" (16:30).

These details align with and confirm what we observed about the Sabbath in Genesis 2:1–3. In both cases, God prescribes to human beings a weekly pattern of six days followed by the seventh. The six days are to be devoted to labor. On the seventh day, people are to refrain from labor. In Exodus 16, God is so committed to this pattern that he provides a double portion of manna on the sixth day to meet Israel's bodily needs on the seventh day. He does not want Israel to be concerned about food or working to get food on the seventh day. Thus, the seventh day is a day of rest—"a day of solemn rest, a holy Sabbath to the LORD" (16:23). However, this day is not marked merely by cessation from labor. It is also a day that is solemn and holy to God, a day that is set apart to his worship. Surely that day would have been characterized by Israel's corporate response of gratitude and devotion to the God who had redeemed them and was leading them in the wilderness.

Though this is the first time that Scripture records an explicit command about the Sabbath, there is no indication in the text that God was giving it to Israel for the very first time. It does come by way of divine command, but it is a command with which Israel appears to have had prior familiarity. The institution of the Sabbath at the creation and the subsequent perpetuation of the Sabbath's observance among the patriarchal generations likely accounts for this familiarity.

Even so, we are told in Exodus that "on the seventh day some of the people went out to gather, but they found none" (16:27). God is displeased with this behavior and tells Moses, "How long will you refuse to keep my commandments and my laws?" (16:28).

The Hebrew verb translated "you refuse" is plural. God, therefore, is speaking to Israel through Moses concerning their disobedience to his "commandments" and "laws." God then reiterates the Sabbath command—"See! The Lord has given you the Sabbath" (16:29). Strikingly, God does not punish the offenders for their transgression; he exercises patience and longsuffering toward Israel at this early stage of their pilgrimage wandering.

The Sabbath at Sinai

The high point in the progress of Old Testament revelation about the Sabbath comes on Mount Sinai. Having led Israel to this mountain, God tells them,

> "You yourselves have seen what I did to the Egyptians, and how I bore you on eagles' wings and brought you to myself. Now therefore, if you will indeed obey my voice and keep my covenant, you shall be my treasured possession among all peoples, for all the earth is mine; and you shall be to me a kingdom of priests and a holy nation." These are the words that you shall speak to the people of Israel. (Ex. 19:4–6)

In other words, God has redeemed Israel from bondage in Egypt, and he calls them to be a special people to himself. As they "obey [God's] voice and keep [his] covenant," they will experience the blessings of life in covenant with God.[1]

The laws that Israel must observe in covenant with God follow, beginning in Exodus 20. These Ten Commandments constitute the

---

1. God is not telling Israel here that their obedience is a procuring precondition for receiving the promises that he makes. Rather, he is explaining how a redeemed people can and must experientially enter into the promises that he has freely given—they must do so by obedience according to the terms of his covenant with them. See further my discussion in *The Lord's Supper as the Sign and Meal of the New Covenant*, Short Studies in Biblical Theology (Wheaton, IL: Crossway, 2019), 27–29.

heart and center of the Mosaic legislation.[2] They are given before any other commandment in this covenant, and they are written upon stone with the finger of God (Ex. 31:18; 34:1). Overall, they provide the moral foundation for the many specific laws and commandments that follow in Exodus through Deuteronomy.[3] And among these Ten Commandments is a command governing the Sabbath. It appears twice in the Pentateuch—in Exodus 20 and, in slightly different form, in Deuteronomy 5. We will look at each to see what God wanted his covenant people to understand about the Sabbath and how they should observe it.

EXODUS 20:8–11

In Exodus 20:8–11, God gives a command relating to the observance of the Sabbath:

> Remember the Sabbath day, to keep it holy. Six days you shall labor, and do all your work, but the seventh day is a Sabbath to the LORD your God. On it you shall not do any work, you, or your son, or your daughter, your male servant, or your female servant, or your livestock, or the sojourner who is within your gates. For in six days the LORD made heaven and earth, the sea, and all that is in them, and rested on the seventh day. Therefore the LORD blessed the Sabbath day and made it holy.

This command and the command that follows (20:12) are unique among the Ten Commandments in that they do not begin with a prohibition. Furthermore, the Sabbath command is the only command

---

2. The phrase "the Ten Commandments" appears at Deuteronomy 10:4. The Hebrew reads, "the ten words."

3. For example, the commandment "You shall not steal" (Ex. 20:15) serves to ground the various Pentateuchal laws governing property, theft, timely wages, usury, and financial restitution (among others).

among the ten that calls Israel to "remember." It also joins the previous two commandments in having grounds or reasons assigned to the commandment.[4]

Overall, it is important to bear in mind that the Sabbath commandment begins with the positive imperative, "remember." God first calls Israel to "remember the Sabbath day, to keep it holy" (20:8). The Sabbath is something that Israel must strive to keep before their mind. They must not allow their observance of it to lapse. In particular, Israel must "remember . . . to keep it holy." The Sabbath is a day that is set apart by God for sacred purposes, and Israel's practice must conform to what God intends for the day.

However, the word "remember" likely does more than summon Israel not to neglect the Sabbath and its observance in the course of their week-to-week existence—God is calling Israel to remember the Sabbath that he instituted at the creation for all people. After all, Exodus 20:11 explicitly references God's creation of the world and in particular makes "a clear reference back to Genesis 2:3."[5] Just as the creation ordinance of labor finds iteration in this commandment ("six days you shall labor"; cf. Gen. 2:15), so does the creation ordinance of Sabbath rest.

Moreover, the contours of this Sabbath commandment align with those of the Sabbath commandment given at creation. In the first place, God tells Israel that he has reserved six days on which they "shall labor." Work is a positive command for human beings. But the labors of the six days must be set down on the "seventh day." On the Sabbath, Israel "shall not do any work"—neither must anyone in an Israelite's household, even a "sojourner" (Ex. 20:10). Israel must keep the day "holy" (20:8), even as God himself has "made it holy"

---

4. In each case (Ex. 20:5–6, 7, 11), the reasons relate to the character and activity of God himself.

5. Gregory K. Beale, *A New Testament Biblical Theology: The Unfolding of the New Testament in the New* (Grand Rapids, MI: Baker, 2011), 781.

(20:11; cf. Gen. 2:3). The Sabbath is a day that God has set apart for his people to gather together in his worship;[6] it is a day that God has uniquely "blessed" (Ex. 20:11; cf. Gen. 2:3). In the context of the covenant that God has made at Mount Sinai with his people, the Sabbath is a day when they will come to enjoy the covenant blessings that God has freely given to them.

So then, the ground or basis of the Sabbath command is God's own activity and design. He worked to create the world and everything in it in six days and then rested on the seventh (Ex. 20:11). This basis tells us at least two things. First, Israel's time is not their own. God exercises the prerogatives of his lordship over his image bearers and therefore Israel must order and allot their time according to the command of God. Second, Israel's worship of God on the Sabbath should spotlight God as the creator of heaven and earth. His power, wisdom, and goodness—all on display in the works of creation—should elicit Israel's praise, adoration, gratitude, and thanksgiving.

DEUTERONOMY 5:12–15

As Israel is poised to enter the promised land after its wilderness wanderings, Moses, whom God has forbidden to enter the land, gives an extended farewell address, found in Deuteronomy. In the course of delivering his final words to Israel, Moses reminds this second generation of the Ten Commandments that God had delivered to their fathers at Sinai. Thus, in Deuteronomy 5:12–15, the Sabbath commandment appears once again, in slightly different form. It reads:

> Observe the Sabbath day, to keep it holy, as the LORD your
> God commanded you. Six days you shall labor and do all

---

6. The association of the Sabbath and God's sanctuary in the laws of Leviticus confirm that the Sabbath is a day set apart for Israel's gathered worship of God (Lev. 19:30; 26:2).

your work, but the seventh day is a Sabbath to the LORD your God. On it you shall not do any work, you or your son or your daughter or your male servant or your female servant, or your ox or your donkey or any of your livestock, or the sojourner who is within your gates, that your male servant and your female servant may rest as well as you. You shall remember that you were a slave in the land of Egypt, and the LORD your God brought you out from there with a mighty hand and an outstretched arm. Therefore the LORD your God commanded you to keep the Sabbath day.

Overall, much of this passage resembles the previous form of the Sabbath command in Exodus 20:8–11. The most notable difference comes in the last verse. In Exodus, God grounds Israel's Sabbath observance in his creation of the world in six days and his resting on the seventh. In Deuteronomy, however, God offers a complementary but distinct ground for Sabbath observance—redemption. Israel had been enslaved in Egypt, and God had redeemed them "with a mighty hand and an outstretched arm" (Deut. 5:15). But what is the connection between Sabbath resting and redemption? The verb translated "labor" in 5:13 and the noun translated "slave" in 5:15 are related in the Hebrew. Thus, the Sabbath, according to Deuteronomy, "was a memorial of [Israel's] redemption out of a toilsome existence into a blessed existence as God's covenant people."[7]

This observation helps to explain an additional detail in Deuteronomy 5:14. Israel is to keep the Sabbath, they are told, so "that your male servant and your female servant may rest as well as you" (cf. Ex. 20:10). In other words, the memory of enslavement in Egypt should prompt Israel not only to set down their own labors on the seventh

---

7. Andrew G. Shead, "Sabbath," in *New Dictionary of Biblical Theology*, ed. T. Desmond Alexander, Brian S. Rosner, D. A. Carson, and Graeme Goldsworthy (Downers Grove, IL: InterVarsity Press, 2000), 747.

day but also to ensure that their servants find "rest as well." In this way, the Sabbath calls Israel to look in two directions. Vertically, they must look to God, their redeemer, from bondage in Egypt. Horizontally, they must look to the physical and spiritual well-being of their own servants. They must free their servants from the demands of this-worldly labor on the seventh day so that these servants, in company with the rest of Israel, may devote the day to the worship of God.

Yet, overall, the primary intention of the redemptive grounds given in Deuteronomy 5:15 was that Israel remember God as their redeemer in the course of their Sabbath worship. The Sabbath was a day to celebrate what God had done to rescue helpless Israel from slavery in Egypt, to remember his power, wisdom, and mercy in redeeming Israel, and to worship him as the God who had entered into covenant with them.

Conclusions

Taken together, the two forms of the Sabbath commandment in Exodus 20 and Deuteronomy 5 lay the foundation for the Sabbath legislation that follows in the Pentateuch. Here, God not only issues the command to rest on the seventh day and to devote it to the worship of God but also gives the reasons for why Israel is to do so. They are to look to God as their creator and redeemer and to dedicate the day to the grateful remembrance of his works of creation and redemption. Further, this day also has important implications for how God's people were to think of themselves in relation to other people. The fact that "sojourners" dwelling in the Israelites' gates were obliged to keep the commandment reinforces worship as the ultimate goal of all humans' existence, whether they be Jew or Gentile (Ex. 20:10). And the fact that servants, whether male or female, were not exempted from this commandment (Deut. 5:14) reinforces their full dignity as image bearers, a point that surfaces again and again in the legislation of the Pentateuch.

With this foundation laid at Sinai, God proceeds to give Israel laws, signs, and specific blessings and curses that uniquely relate to Israel's calling as God's covenant people under the Mosaic covenant. In the remainder of this chapter, we will look at four particular and distinct ways that the Sabbath resurfaces in these connections. In exploring them, we will see not only how God wants his people to look back to the works that he has already done but also how God wants his people to look ahead in anticipation of work that he has yet to accomplish, namely, salvation in Christ.

Sabbath and Sign

In Exodus, God speaks of the Sabbath as "sign," saying, "Above all you shall keep my Sabbaths, for this is a sign between me and you throughout your generations, that you may know that I, the Lord, sanctify you" (Ex. 31:12) and "It is a sign forever between me and the people of Israel that in six days the Lord made heaven and earth, and on the seventh day he rested and was refreshed" (31:17). Here, when God calls the Sabbath a "sign," he has in mind the covenant that he made with Israel at Sinai when he said, "Therefore the people of Israel shall keep the Sabbath, observing the Sabbath throughout their generations, as a covenant forever. It is a sign forever" (31:16–17). The Sabbath, then, is a sign of the Mosaic covenant: "As the Noahic covenant has a 'sign' (Gen. 9:13, 17) in the rainbow and the Abrahamic covenant has a 'sign' (Gen. 17:11) in circumcision, so the Sinai covenant has a 'sign' in the sabbath."[8] Later, under the new covenant, both baptism and the Lord's Supper will serve as covenant signs.[9]

---

8. Gerhard F. Hasel, "Sabbath," in *Anchor Bible Dictionary*, ed. David Noel Freedman (New York: Doubleday, 1992), 5:852.

9. Hasel, "Sabbath," 5:852.

Overall, the purpose of a covenant sign is to display in tangible, physical form the promises promulgated in a particular covenant. The rainbow, for instance, was a sign of God's promise never again to "destroy all flesh" by "a flood" of "waters" (Gen. 9:15).[10] In similar fashion, the Sabbath visibly displays the promises of God given under the Mosaic covenant.

If we were to ask which promises the Sabbath represents, the answer is found in Exodus 31:17 and 13. In the first place, the Sabbath is a sign pointing Israel to creation, specifically, that God made the world in six days, rested the seventh, and found rest and refreshment on that seventh day (Ex. 31:17). Thus, God is doing more than offering Israel a weekly reminder of the historical fact of the creation of the world. As we have seen in our studies of Genesis 2:1–3 and Exodus 20:8–11, his six days of work followed by one day of rest constitutes a standing pattern for humanity's ordering of time. That seventh day was not only to be a day of physical resting from the labors of the six days but also—and primarily—to be a holy resting. The Sabbath is a day of worship and spiritual resting, a day to receive the blessings that God particularly promises to those who draw near to him in worship on that day. The Sabbath served as a sign, then, of God's continuing intention and willingness to bless and spiritually refresh his covenant people when they drew near to him in weekly Sabbath worship. As took take up God's challenge to lay down their weekly labors for one day each week, they had a reminder in the Sabbath itself that great spiritual blessings lay ahead of them and that God was wholeheartedly willing to grant them.

In the second place, the Sabbath is a sign pointing Israel to redemption, specifically, says God, "that you may know that I, the LORD,

---

10. While certainly intended for human beings to behold and to be reminded of God's pledge not to destroy the world again by a flood of water, God expressly says that he will behold that sign and remember his covenant promises (Gen. 9:16).

sanctify you" (Ex. 31:13). The holy God had "made" the seventh day "holy" (Gen. 2:3; Ex. 20:11). And he had called his redeemed people to be a "holy nation" (Ex. 19:6; cf. Lev. 20:26). Thus, the Sabbath is not merely a sign testifying to the holiness of God, the holiness of the seventh day, or the calling of Israel as the holy people of God—it is also a sign of God's pledge to "sanctify" his people, that is, to *make* them holy (cf. Lev. 21:8). God, in other words, has committed himself to making his people, by grace, into what he has called them to be. The Sabbath day plays a special role in this project—it is a reminder of God's gracious commitment to make his people holy. Just as importantly, it is the occasion on which God, meeting with his covenant people in worship, makes them holy by grace. As the Sabbath points to these gracious realities, it serves as a covenant sign to Israel.

However, we should note that while the Sabbath is a sign of the Mosaic covenant, it is not only a sign of the Mosaic covenant. Its foundations lie in the creation itself and, as such, touches on all human beings in all times and places of the world. Its "sign" dimension under the Mosaic covenant lends to the Sabbath an added layer of meaning, one that is unique to the people of God under the Mosaic covenant. However, when the Mosaic covenant (and its signs) expire with the dawning of the new covenant, the Sabbath does not altogether expire. Its function as a sign of the Mosaic covenant certainly ceases. But, as a creation ordinance, the Sabbath has continuing significance in the life of humanity. Even so, the "sign" character of the Mosaic Sabbath helps us to appreciate the way in which the entire history of redemption moves toward its goal, the saving work of the last Adam.

Sabbath and Sanctions

A second way that the Sabbath surfaces uniquely within the Mosaic covenant is through the sanctions that are associated with breaking it. In the passage we explored above (Ex. 31:12–17), God threatens the breakers of the Sabbath with capital punishment, saying,

> You shall keep the Sabbath, because it is holy for you. Everyone who profanes it shall be put to death. Whoever does any work on it, that soul shall be cut off from among his people. Six days shall work be done, but the seventh day is a Sabbath of solemn rest, holy to the LORD. Whoever does any work on the Sabbath day shall be put to death (Ex. 31:14–15).

Later in the Pentateuch, in Numbers 15:32–36, we see this sanction implemented. An Israelite is discovered "gathering sticks on the Sabbath day" (Num. 15:32; cf. Ex. 35:3). By God's express direction, the man is sentenced to death by congregational stoning "outside the camp" (Num. 15:35), and the sentence is carried out according to God's command (15:36).

Overall, God communicates several important points about the Sabbath by adding this sanction and commanding its execution in the case of the man found gathering sticks on the Sabbath. The first is that God deems the breaking of the Sabbath in Israel to be a "profan[ing]" of the day (Ex. 31:14). God has made the day holy, and to break the express command of the Sabbath by engaging in work that belongs to the six days is to defile or profane the day. This sanction, then, is a testimony to the regard in which God holds the Sabbath as a holy day, set apart from work and for worship. The second point is that the violation of this law of God carries with it the sentence of death. This association of sin and death is not new. God had threatened death if Adam sinned against him by eating the forbidden fruit (Gen. 2:16–17), Adam did sin, and death was the result. In Exodus 31:14–15, as in other passages (cf. Lev. 24:10–16), the Mosaic legislation reinforces the principle that "the soul who sins shall die" or, in other words, "the wages of sin is death" (Ezek. 18:4;

Rom. 6:23). Last, the third point appears from the fact that the execution happens "outside the camp" (Num. 15:35), which implies that the violator is "cut off from among his people" (Ex. 31:14). The covenant community is the place where God makes covenant blessing available to people, so to be placed outside the camp is therefore to be relegated to the realm of curse.

So what is God intending to communicate to Israel through these civil penalties? The infliction of the death penalty is no certain sign that an Israelite was an unbeliever, only that he had committed an offense deserving the prescribed penalty. Thus, God is intending to teach his people important lessons about sin: to sin against God's law is a profaning act; sin deserves eternal death; sin deserves eternal curse. The Mosaic penalties were imaging on a temporal level the nature and consequences of sin at the eternal level.

This principle is further developed in later revelation. When writing the churches in Galatia, Paul tells us that every human being who fails to keep even one command of God's law is justly under the curse of God (Gal. 3:10). For this reason, no one can be counted righteous by law keeping (3:11). After all, no sinner can see eternal life by perfect law keeping (3:12). The good news of the gospel is that Christ "redeemed us from the curse of the law by becoming a curse for us" (3:13). He who was entirely righteous "was cut off out of the land of the living, stricken for the transgression of [God's] people" (Isa. 53:8). Even though we all "like sheep have gone astray," Isaiah tells us, "the LORD has laid on him the iniquity of us all" (53:6). Jesus "suffered outside the gate in order to sanctify the people through his own blood" (Heb. 13:12). Thus, the Mosaic law, and particularly its penal sanctions, were pointing Israel to the coming of God's Messiah who would be unjustly condemned by the Jewish leadership as a blasphemer (Mark 14:64) and die an accursed death outside the city of Jerusalem—all to redeem sinners from their sins by his blood.

Sabbath and Seasons

A third way that the Sabbath appears within the Mosaic laws concerns the calendar of worship that God gave Israel to follow. Israel was to worship God only in the ways that God had expressly authorized in his word; any unauthorized worship was thereby forbidden to them. One of God's prescriptions for worship concerned the time of worship. We have already seen that the Ten Commandments require one day in seven to be set apart for Israel's worship of God, but God also called Israel to worship him on additional occasions. These occasions occurred regularly over the course of a calendar year—Israel's weeks, months, and years were structured by set dates when they were to gather in order to worship God.

God gives Israel a calendar of worship in Leviticus 23. And the cornerstone of the calendar is the weekly Sabbath—verse 3 reads, "Six days shall work be done, but on the seventh day is a Sabbath of solemn rest, a holy convocation. You shall do no work. It is a Sabbath to the LORD in all your dwelling places." In sum, Israel has "solemn rest" and does "no work" on the seventh day, the Sabbath, which is to be a day of "holy convocation," a gathering in public assembly to worship God; this must be done "in all [her] dwelling places." Thus, Israel would gather in many local assemblies across the land each Sabbath in order to worship God, which is when special offerings would also be presented at the tabernacle (see Num. 28:9–10).

God then appoints an annual cycle of feasts, beginning in the spring and continuing through the fall—Passover (Lev. 23:4–8), Firstfruits (23:9–14), Weeks (23:15–22), Trumpets (23:23–25), the Day of Atonement (23:26–32), and Booths (23:33–43). Strikingly, aspects of these feasts resemble the celebration of the weekly Sabbath. Passover, Weeks, and Trumpets involve "holy convocations" on which Israel must "not do any ordinary work" (23:4, 7, 8, 21, 24–25). The first day of Booths is "a holy convocation," and the last day, "a solemn assembly"; on neither of these may "any ordinary work" be done (23:35, 36). God calls the Day of Atonement "a Sabbath of solemn rest" on which the Israelites are to "afflict themselves" (23:32; cf. 23:39). Booths is as celebratory as the Day of Atonement is somber; on the first day of Booths, God tells Israel to observe their "solemn rest" by "rejoic[ing] before the LORD your God seven days" (23:40).

Thus, God appoints a plurality of sabbaths beyond the weekly Sabbath to fill Israel's annual calendar of worship. In each case, he calls Israel to lay down their work, to gather in public assembly, and to worship him. On the Day of Atonement, the mood is appropriately somber, even as Booths is characterized by joyful celebration. These "sabbaths," unique to Israel's life under the Mosaic covenant, serve to complement Israel's weekly worship of God on the Sabbath day.

There is one additional layer to the recurring cycle of Israel's worship. In Leviticus 25, God appoints a Sabbath year to fall every seventh year (25:1–7) as well as a jubilee year to fall every fiftieth year after seven cycles of seven years have been completed (25:8–17). He declares the Sabbath year to be "a Sabbath of solemn rest for the land, a Sabbath to the LORD" (25:4) and forbids Israel from sowing the fields or reaping what may grow in them and from pruning their vineyards or gathering the fruit of their vineyards (25:4–5). Yet, he promises that "the Sabbath of the land shall provide food" for the entire human and animal population of Israel (25:6–7; cf. 25:18–22). Not only people and livestock but also the land itself was to enjoy and benefit from the seventh-year Sabbath rest that God appointed for Israel. Thus, "the sabbatical year reinforced the fact that Israel had been set apart by God for rest (Lev. 25:12) . . . [and] even the land itself was only a foretaste of what God had promised."[11]

---

11. Shead, "Sabbath," 747.

The jubilee year is not termed a sabbath, but it shares certain features with the multiple sabbaths that God had appointed in the Mosaic calendar. Like the Sabbath year, the jubilee year brought the land added rest as Israel was "neither [to] sow nor reap what grows of itself nor gather the grapes from the undressed vines" (25:11). And, like the sabbaths of Israel's annual calendar, the jubilee was to be "holy" to Israel (25:12). But, uniquely, the jubilee was chiefly designed to celebrate the liberty that was the birthright of God's covenant people. Israelites were to return to their ancestral properties and take possession of them if, for some reason during the previous fifty years, that property had been sold to another party (25:10, cf. 25:13–17). Thus, in this way, Israel's liberty came to expression as inheritances were restored to Israelites who may have been separated from them in previous years. This liberty, of course, fundamentally distinguished Israel's present condition in the land from their past bondage in Egypt and therefore provided a critical link between Israel's weekly Sabbath celebrations and their celebration of the jubilee year (cf. Deut. 5:15).

In summary, Israel's calendar of worship reinforced the weekly Sabbath in some important ways. The occasional, recurring feasts called Israel to cease from their work and to gather to worship God for some specific purpose, whether to celebrate God's work of redemption in the exodus (Passover), God's provision in the harvest (Weeks), and God's care for Israel in the wilderness (Booths), or to mourn for sin and to look to God for pardon (Day of Atonement). The Feast of Weeks, the Sabbatical year, and the jubilee were all calculated in units of seven. All in all, these recurring patterns surely would have reinforced the importance and significance of the weekly Sabbath.[12]

---

12. Jay Sklar, *Leviticus: An Introduction and Commentary,* Tyndale Old Testament Commentaries (Downers Grove, IL: InterVarsity Press, 2014), 277, cited at L. Michael Morales, *Who*

Further, the Sabbath year and the jubilee required Israel to cease agricultural labors for an extended period of time. God challenges Israel to trust him that "the land will yield its fruit, and you will eat your fill and dwell in it securely" (Lev. 25:19). Such recurring experiences would have impressed upon Israel that the land was God's free gift to them and that it was God himself who was providing for Israel through the land. In particular, it would have served as an ongoing reminder to Israel that the land was only a pointer to the rest held out to them in the weekly Sabbath, the festival sabbaths, the Sabbath year, and the jubilee. Thus, Israel's calendar of worship was designed to remind Israel again and again of the heavenly rest of worship and communion with God that belongs to each child of God.

Sabbath and Subsequent History

A fourth and final observation is that the Sabbath institution—with all the covenant blessings and curses attached to it under the Mosaic covenant—helps to shape the contours of future events in the life of God's covenant people, Israel. As the New Testament stresses, God designed the Mosaic law to point Israel to the Savior whom he had promised to send as the redeemer of his elect in every age (Gal. 3:24). Thus the Pentateuch both asks and answers the question, "Will Israel in fact trust and obey the God who has redeemed them, taken them into covenant with him, and is preparing them for the arrival of the Savior of the world?" It does so in part by giving us hints of what would come next in Israel's history—they would be removed from the land, under the curse of the covenant, for their unbelief and disobedience.

The Sabbath, in particular, surfaces in this depiction of Israel's future. In Leviticus 26, God outlines the blessings and the curses that

---

Shall Ascend the Mountain of the Lord: A Biblical Theology of the Book of Leviticus, New Studies in Biblical Theology 37 (Downers Grove, IL: InterVarsity Press, 2015), 190.

attend his covenant with Israel—blessings for faith and obedience, curses for unbelief and disobedience. The amount of time that God devotes to outlining the curses threatened for disobedience portends their implementation in Israel's future (Lev. 26:14–45). Overall, God pledges to remove Israel from the land, "scatter[ing them] among the nations" and leaving the "land" a "desolation" (26:33). At that point, God says, "the land shall enjoy its Sabbaths as long as it lies desolate, while you are in your enemies' land; then the land shall rest, and enjoy its Sabbaths. As long as it lies desolate it shall have rest, the rest that it did not have on your Sabbaths when you were dwelling in it" (26:34–35; cf. 26:43).

Thus, God indicates that Israel will disregard the sabbaths that he has appointed for the land in his law. This speaks to a disregard for God's covenant and its commands; in particular, it testifies to a steadfast disregard for the worship that God had appointed in his law. As a result, Israel will come under the curse of the covenant and be removed from the land. But thankfully, this is not God's last word. He pledges that if Israel confesses their sins, he will remember his covenant (26:40–42); even as they languish in exile, he will not "destroy them utterly and break [his] covenant with them" (26:44; cf. 26:45).

To trace the further history of Israel, we need to look to the biblical books that chronicle that history, particularly to the prophets whom God raised up to speak words of judgment and restoration to his people. As we turn to that period of redemptive history, we will catch some important glimpses of the Sabbath that will help us to understand it more clearly and fully. Perhaps most importantly, the prophets help us to see more and more how the Sabbath relates to the work of the coming Messiah, the Son of God, Jesus Christ.

3

Prophets

In many ways, the prophets are the public prosecutors of the Old Testament. God appoints them to bring charges against Israel for their violations of God's covenant charter, the Mosaic law. It is no surprise, then, that violations of the Sabbath feature in the prophets' denunciations of Israel's stubborn and persistent law-breaking. However, the prophets are no less beacons of hope. They look past impending judgment of an impenitent and disobedient Israel to a glorious future restoration. This restoration will come about when God sends his Son, the Messiah, to save sinners from every nation; it will include Jews but it will also encompass people from every nation. Thus, just as the Sabbath features in prophetic words of judgment to Israel, so also the Sabbath features in the prophetic vision of restoration in Christ. In this chapter, we will explore three prophets' testimonies to the Sabbath. We will then look at one of the last books in the Old Testament, Nehemiah. Nehemiah shows us that even though Israel had returned to the land after their exile, the restoration promised in the prophets still lay ahead. In all of these ways, the Old Testament propels us toward its goal, the person and work of the Lord Jesus Christ.

Isaiah

Isaiah prophesied during the eighth century BC in the southern kingdom (Judah). His ministry was one by which God largely hardened the prophet's contemporaries (Isa. 6:8–10). But in the aftermath of the judgment that was to come upon Israel for their sins, God would preserve a remnant, from which would come the Messiah (6:13). Much of Isaiah's later chapters concentrate on the glorious ministry of God's servant, whose suffering would redeem a multitude from among the nations (see especially 52:13–53:12). And this saving work of the servant would usher the redeemed into the glorious rest of the new creation (see especially 65:1–66:24).

Overall, much of Isaiah's ministry is dedicated to calling Israel to account for their sins. In the opening chapter, God indicts Israel for approaching him on the "new moon and Sabbath and the calling of convocations" (1:13). The reason that God is displeased with Israel's adherence to the law's calendar of worship is that they approach God with "hands . . . full of blood" (1:15). When they gather in the assembly of worship, they bring "the evil of [their] deeds . . . before [God's] eyes" (1:16). For this reason, God says, "I cannot endure iniquity and solemn assembly" (1:13). Their worship has "become a burden" to God, and he is "weary of bearing" it (1:14). Israel's has paired their ceremonial scrupulosity with moral depravity. This makes a mockery of God's intentions for worship; the worship that is acceptable to God is offered from a heart that is dedicated to putting off evil and pursuing good (see 1:16–17).

It is no surprise, then, that worship features prominently in the oracles of restoration that come in the latter part of Isaiah's prophecy. Three passages in particular highlight the place of the Sabbath in the future hope that Isaiah presents before us—Isaiah 56:1–8, 58:13–14, and 66:23. Each passage distinctly shows how God will not only remove sin and its effects from his people but also bring to consummation the purposes for humanity that he announced at creation.

Isaiah 56:1–8

In Isaiah 55, God freely invites sinners to come to him to receive the salvation that he alone provides (55:1–13). This chapter closes with a promise that the redeemed "shall go out in joy and be led forth in peace" (55:12), and the next, Isaiah 56, opens with a call to await patiently the fullness of the Lord's promised "salvation" and "righteousness" as well as to "keep justice, and do righteousness" in the meantime (56:1). God then explains what this justice and righteousness look like, describing them in terms of Sabbath keeping and refraining from evil (56:2).

In particular, God pronounces his blessing upon "the man . . . who keeps the Sabbath, not profaning it" (56:2). Strikingly, this blessing is not restricted to the Jew. It belongs to any human being who observes and does not profane the Sabbath. That this blessing is not the possession of any particular segment of humanity is confirmed by what God says in subsequent verses. He clarifies that "the foreigner who has joined himself to the Lord" and the "eunuch" have a place among his people (56:3). And so, "to the eunuchs who keep [his] Sabbaths, who choose the things that please [him] and hold fast [his] covenant," God promises an "everlasting name" (56:4, 5). To "the foreigners who join themselves to the Lord . . . everyone who keeps the Sabbath and does not profane it, and holds fast [his] covenant," God pledges to "bring" them to his "holy mountain" and to accept their worship (56:6, 7). God, then, will ingather not only "the outcasts of Israel" (56:8) but also eunuchs and Gentiles. God will redeem people from across the human race. He will bring them within the bounds of his covenant, and they will keep the Sabbath, offering the worship that he created them—and redeemed them—to offer to him.

From this oracle a clear picture of Sabbath observance emerges—the Sabbath is preeminently characterized by the gathered worship of God's people. In sum, this worship has at least three features. First, it is marked by the proclamation of God's word. God will draw people to his "holy mountain" (56:7). It will be to this mountain, Isaiah has told us earlier, that "all the nations shall flow" and where God will "teach" them "his ways . . . that [they] may walk in his paths" (2:2, 3). The "law" and the "word of the LORD" will proceed from there (2:3). Second, God terms this place of worship a "house of prayer for all peoples" where his redeemed will be "joyful" (56:7). As God speaks to his people from his word in worship, his people speak to him in prayer. Third, this worship will also be characterized by "burnt offerings and . . . sacrifices" on the "altar" of God (56:7). Sinners find acceptance and joy in the presence of God by his appointed sacrifice. A few chapters earlier, God highlighted the servant's sin-bearing, sacrificial death on behalf of sinners (see 53:4–6, 7, 10, 12). The worship of the redeemed in Isaiah 56, then, finds the priestly work of Christ as its centerpiece. Sinners from among the nations draw near to God and offer acceptable worship in the name and by the merits of their heavenly high priest.

Clearly, this worship is vertical in its orientation. However, it also has an indispensable horizontal component. The redeemed not only "keeps the Sabbath, not profaning it," but he "keeps his hand from doing any evil" (56:2). Furthermore, Sabbath keeping is paired with "hold[ing] fast [God's] covenant" (56:4, 6). The problem identified in Isaiah 1—ceremonial piety coupled with moral impurity—will no longer plague God's people. The true worship of God will be paired with a universal commitment to righteousness among their fellow human beings. In this way, the redeemed will enjoy life in covenant with God.

Tellingly, Jesus quotes Isaiah 56:7 ("for my house shall be called a house of prayer for all peoples") when he cleanses the temple at the close of his ministry (Matt. 21:12–17; Mark 11:15–18). This implies that the temple that was rebuilt after the restoration of Judah to the land under the Persians did not witness the complete fulfillment of Isaiah's prophecy. In this passage, Jesus particularly indicts his Jewish contemporaries for having made the temple a "den of robbers" (Mark 11:17); the Jewish nation is like a leafy tree that promises fruit but is in fact fruitless (see 11:12–14, 20–25). As we will later see, the death and resurrection of Christ will mark a needed transformation in this worship. Only in the risen Jesus Christ, the true temple of God, will the nations offer God the worship that Isaiah describes here.

Isaiah 58:13–14

The next two chapters continue Isaiah's concern for worship. Here, God indicts Israel for their idolatry (57:1–13) and for fasting without concern for repentance (58:1–12). Then, he sets forth the kind of righteousness that should accompany true worship, emphasizing the spiritual blessing that he promises to give to those who pursue this righteousness (58:5–12). Last, in Isaiah 58:13–14, God turns to addressing how Israel should observe the Sabbath. In doing so, he "set[s] the feast [of the Sabbath] over against the fast."[1] He says:

> If you turn back your foot from the Sabbath,
>   from doing your pleasure on my holy day,
> and call the Sabbath a delight
>   and the holy day of the LORD honorable;
> if you honor it, not going your own ways,
>   or seeking your own pleasure, or talking idly;
> then you shall take delight in the LORD,
>   and I will make you ride on the heights of the earth;

---

1. Alec Motyer, *The Prophecy of Isaiah: An Introduction & Commentary* (Downers Grove, IL: InterVarsity Press, 1993), 483.

I will feed you with the heritage of Jacob your father,
for the mouth of the LORD has spoken.

In other words, God challenges Israel to refrain from doing what they want to do, going where they want to go, and talking about what they want to talk about on *his* day. Whether in speech or in behavior, Israel has made the Sabbath a vehicle for pursuing their own interests and pleasures. Instead, God tells Israel to honor and delight in his Sabbath. This challenge hinges on "whose 'pleasure' or 'desire' (cf. 58:2, 3) is going to dictate the life pattern of the people—Yahweh's or their own?"[2] Thus, God calls Israel to observe the Sabbath by pursuing what pleases him rather than what pleases them.

As he did in his earlier challenge concerning fasting, God promises blessing to those who take up his challenge to observe the Sabbath in the way that pleases him. By setting aside their own pleasures and doing what delights God, they will find delight in him. Further, God pledges to make them "ride on the heights of the earth" and to "feed [them] with the heritage of Jacob [their] father," a reference to Deuteronomy 32:13, in which God recounts his covenant blessings to Israel when he brought them into the land. Thus, God is promising rich covenantal blessing in connection with this Sabbath observance. Those who keep the Sabbath holy and draw near to him in worship on that day, God says, will find for themselves pleasure and covenant blessing—the very matters to which the Sabbath had pointed from the creation (see Gen. 2:1–3).

ISAIAH 66:23

Isaiah's prophecy closes with a panoramic vision of the restored creation, the new heavens and new earth (see Isa. 65:17; 66:22). After

---

2. John L. Mackay, *Isaiah, Volume 2: Chapters 40-66* (Darlington, UK: Evangelical Press, 2009), 463.

an oracle of God's judgment, particularly upon those who participate in false worship (66:15–17), God pledges to "gather all nations and tongues. And they shall come and shall see [his] glory" (66:18). They will come to his "holy mountain Jerusalem" and they will offer worship that is acceptable (66:20). God promises that as the new creation "shall remain," so also "shall [Israel's] offspring and . . . name remain" (66:22). Nothing will disrupt the security of God's people, gathered to him in worship.

In the next verse, God says that worship will be offered to him continually in the new creation: "From new moon to new moon, and from Sabbath to Sabbath, all flesh shall come to worship before me, declares the Lord" (66:23). Here, "all flesh" refers to all kinds of human beings, whether Jew or Gentile, and the reference to the "new moon" and "Sabbath" points back to the very beginning of Isaiah's prophecy ("New moon and Sabbath and the calling of convocations—I cannot endure iniquity and solemn assembly" [1:13]). But whereas God formerly loathed Israel's observance of the new moon and Sabbath, now he accepts the worship of "all flesh" in the new creation.

Thus, in this passage God emphasizes that worship will be a hallmark of the new creation. "New moon" and "Sabbath" were times appointed by God for his people's worship of him at the beginning of each lunar month and the end of each calendar week respectively. Since the observance of each was regulated under the Mosaic covenant, one might argue that God is simply speaking to his people of worship in the new creation in the mere form of these Mosaic laws. As the "new moon" of the Old Testament law will surely not continue into the new creation, so also, one might reason, the Sabbath would not continue into the new creation. But the two festivals are likely yoked here to underscore the way in which God will bring people from corrupted worship (1:13) to restored worship (66:23).[3] Isaiah 56 and 58 have already pointed to a significance the Sabbath has that the "new moon" does not in the restoration prophecies.[4] And the Sabbath, unlike the "new moon," is an ordinance of the creation (Gen. 2:1–3). For these reasons, we may conclude that Isaiah points to the Sabbath as an abiding component of the new creation.[5] In Christ, God will draw men and women from all nations to himself. As they gather to worship him according to the ways of his appointment and not according to their own desires, they will experience rich, covenant blessings. These blessings will come upon them precisely as and because they abide in the presence of God himself. In Christ, God's purposes for humanity in creation come to glorious realization for the people of God in the new creation.

Jeremiah

Jeremiah served a century or so after Isaiah. Sadly, the spiritual condition of the southern kingdom had not improved in the interim. Thus, Jeremiah's prophecies are perched on the hinge of Judah's exile at the hands of the Babylonians in the early sixth century BC. Some oracles take place during the exile but many come in the generation or two leading up to the exile. As one might expect, these prophecies are overwhelmingly words of threatened judgment against Judah for their violations of God's covenant with them.

For example, in Jeremiah 17:19–27, God addresses violations of the Sabbath among the people of Judah and Jerusalem. Positively, God tells his people to "keep the Sabbath holy, as I commanded your fathers" (Jer. 17:22). This reference to Exodus 20:8 ("Remember the Sabbath day, to

---

3. Andrew G. Shead, "Sabbath," in *New Dictionary of Biblical Theology*, ed. T. Desmond Alexander, Brian S. Rosner, D. A. Carson, and Graeme Goldsworthy (Downers Grove, IL: InterVarsity Press,: 2000), 748.

4. The new moon festival is only mentioned twice in Isaiah (1:13, 66:23).

5. For a treatment of the related text, Colossians 2:16–17, see my discussion in chapter 5.

keep it holy") underscores the covenantal context of this command, and the expression "as I commanded your fathers" appears earlier in Jeremiah, referring to the Mosaic covenant (see Jer. 11:4).[6] Consequently, the judgments that God threatens in this passage should be taken as covenantal judgments. But, no less, the promised blessings that God holds out through Jeremiah should be taken as covenantal blessings.

At the beginning of this passage, God sends his prophet to the city gates, particularly to "the People's Gate, by which the kings of Judah enter and by which they go out" (17:19). Jeremiah is commanded to address both "kings of Judah" and the inhabitants of Judah and Jerusalem (17:20). God tells them, "Do not bear a burden on the Sabbath day or bring it in by the gates of Jerusalem. And do not carry a burden out of your houses on the Sabbath or do any work, but keep the Sabbath day holy, as I commanded your fathers" (17:21–22). This shows us that Judah, with the knowledge and likely approval of their kings, habitually violates the Sabbath by engaging in commerce on that day (see Amos 8:5).[7] Sadly, they are perpetuating a practice that has long characterized the people of God—their "fathers . . . did not listen or incline their ear, but stiffened their neck, that they might not hear and receive instruction" (Jer. 17:22–23). The fact that Judah has disobeyed the express letter of the Sabbath command, with resistance and persistence, underscores the seriousness of their situation before God.

God then proposes to Judah either blessing (17:24–26) or curse (17:27). If they "keep the Sabbath day holy and do no work on it" (17:24), two blessings will follow. The first is that Davidic "kings and princes" will enter these gates on "chariots" and "horses," accompanied by their royal retinue (17:25). God will bless the Davidic line with generations of rule. Furthermore, people will come from all over

---

6. John L. Mackay, *Jeremiah: An Introduction and Commentary, Volume 1: Chapters 1-20* (Fearn, UK: Mentor, 2004), 527.

7. In Amos, the prophet quotes people in Israel bemoaning the Sabbath as a burden impeding their commerce, a commerce that is also unjust and oppresses the poor (see Amos 8:4–6).

Judah, bringing multiple sacrifices and offerings to the "house of the LORD" (17:26). There will be an ingathering of God's people from all corners of the land so that they might worship God together. All in all, this picture is one of flourishing, both temporally and spiritually. If Judah listens to God and obeys his command, they will experience the blessings of the covenant—strength, security, and true worship.

But, on the other hand, if Israel disobeys God's command "to keep the Sabbath day holy, and not to bear a burden and enter by the gates of Jerusalem on the Sabbath day," then covenant curse will follow (17:27). God will "kindle a fire" in these gates. That fire will consume the "palaces of Jerusalem and shall not be quenched" (17:27); it will be an expression of God's wrath against his people's sin (see 7:20). The city's gates and palaces, which stand for the economic and royal well-being and prosperity of Judah, will be destroyed in covenant judgment.

The outcome, of course, was the latter—Judah came under the judgment of God for their disobedience to the Mosaic covenant, not least its Sabbath commandments. Significantly, there is in this passage no explicit promise of restoration beyond judgment. Implicitly, however, God associates covenant blessing with the honoring of the Sabbath. In other words, any conceivable restoration for God's people will entail covenant blessings experienced through the observance of the Sabbath. This association between blessing and the Sabbath is precisely what we have seen in Isaiah's prophecies. And it is also what we see in Ezekiel's prophecies.

Ezekiel

Ezekiel was roughly a contemporary of the prophet Jeremiah, but he is unusual among the prophets in that he was also a priest (Ezek. 1:3). It is no surprise, then, that such priestly concerns as the temple and Israel's worship should surface repeatedly throughout Ezekiel's prophecies. Overall, this book is bracketed by the glory of God departing from the temple because of Israel's idolatry (Ezek. 8–10) and the glory of God returning to an eschatological temple in which the true worship of God has been restored (Ezek. 40–48). In between these bookends, Ezekiel's prophecies thus highlight the Sabbath as the spiritual marker of both Israel's abandonment of God's worship and God's eschatological restoration of worship among his people.

For example, in Ezekiel 20:5–31, God rehearses the history of Israel across several distinct periods of time—Israel during their bondage in Egypt (20:5–9), the first wilderness generation (20:10–17), the second wilderness generation (20:18–26), and Israel during their tenure in the land of promise (20:27–31). There are several constants in each era—God shows mercy to Israel; Israel turns from God to idols; God restrains his righteous anger against his sinful people.[8] And as God recounts his dealings with the two wilderness generations, he mentions his "Sabbaths" on several occasions (20:12, 13, 16, 20, 21, 24).

Importantly, "Sabbaths" appears each time in the plural. In view, then, is more than the weekly Sabbath. This term includes the various sabbaths that appear throughout the calendar of worship that God gave Israel in the Pentateuch. God terms these sabbaths "a sign between me and them, that they may know that I am the LORD who sanctifies them" (20:12; cf. 20:20). Here, the term "sign" captures the expressly covenantal significance that the Sabbath took on under the Mosaic covenant. The Sabbath was an indicator of the blessed eternal rest that God had prepared for all who had put their trust in him; it pointed to God's commitment to make his people holy and to their calling as the holy people of God.[9]

---

8. See the helpful synoptic chart at Christopher J. H. Wright, *The Message of Ezekiel,* The Bible Speaks Today (Downers Grove, IL: InterVarsity Press, 2001), 157.

9. See Patrick Fairbairn, *Ezekiel and the Book of His Prophecy: An Exposition* (Edinburgh: T&T Clark, 1855), 217–18.

But Israel rejected these sabbaths. They turned away from God's "statutes" and "rules" and "greatly profaned" his "Sabbaths" (20:13; cf. 20:16, 21). "Their heart went after their idols" (20:16), and "their eyes were set on their fathers' idols" (20:24). In other words, idolatry was transmitted generationally and was a matter of Israel's heart commitments and desires. Thus, it was in light of this steadfast rejection of God's law, and particularly his sabbaths, that God gave Israel over to the idolatry that they desired (20:25–29).[10] God singled out his sabbaths because, as a sign of the Mosaic covenant, Israel's profanation of God's sabbaths signaled their covenant treachery.[11]

Later, the historical survey in Ezekiel 23 of Israel's and Judah's unfaithfulness to God and his covenant also highlights Israel's Sabbath desecration as among their "abominations" (23:36)—God says, "they have defiled my sanctuary on the same day and profaned my Sabbaths" (23:38; cf. Lev 19:30). The holy space and the holy days that God set apart for Israel in his law, Israel has polluted and treated in vain.

Sadly, they did not repent of this sin. In Ezekiel 22, God stresses that Sabbath profanation remains a problem in the days of the prophet. The people "have despised [God's] holy things and profaned [his] Sabbaths" (Ezek. 22:8). In doing so, they have the example of the priests themselves before them; God says, "Her priests have done violence to my law and have profaned my holy things . . . they have disregarded my Sabbaths, so that I am profaned among them" (22:26). Shockingly, the guardians and custodians of God's sabbaths have themselves sinned in this area. The result is that God is "profaned" among his own priests, whom he called to be holy in Israel.

---

10. In verse 25, God does not identify the laws of Torah as the "statutes that were not good and rules by which they could not have life." These "statutes" and "rules," rather, refer to the crushing demands of idol worship that Israel preferred to God's worship and that God, in his providence, permitted Israel to pursue.

11. Gerhard F. Hasel, "Sabbath," in *Anchor Bible Dictionary*, ed. David Noel Freedman (New York: Doubleday, 1992), 5:852–53.

Overall, the testimony of Ezekiel 16, 20, 23, and 22 points to the longstanding profanation of God's sabbaths as a sin that has roused the anger and wrath of God against his people. They have preferred the service of idols to the worship of God. They have coupled the defiling of God's temple with the profanation of his sabbaths. Both the people and the priests are guilty of these sins. And what makes the breaking of God's sabbaths so egregious is that they were the appointed sign of the covenant that God had made with Israel at Sinai. In rejecting God's sabbaths, they were rejecting the covenant of God and the God of the covenant.

Thus, the oracles of restoration that fill the latter portion of Ezekiel are as marvelous as they are unexpected. In place of wicked shepherds, God will raise up a Davidic shepherd, and God himself will shepherd his sheep (34:23, 15). God will solve the problem of Israel's wicked rebellion and rejection of his laws by giving his people a new heart and setting his Spirit within them (36:26, 27).[12] Israel had broken covenant with God, but God will make an everlasting covenant of peace with his people, such that he will dwell with them as their God (37:26, 27). This latter promise to be their God is tied to his promise to "set [his] sanctuary in their midst forevermore" (37:26, 28).

In sum, Ezekiel's vision of this eschatological temple (Ezek. 40–48) is a visible and tangible display of God's commitment to dwell with his people and to bless them as "the LORD who sanctifies Israel" (37:28). At God's direction, Ezekiel describes the architecture and contents of the temple (40:1–43:17), the restored worship that takes place in the temple (43:18–46:24), and the way in which the temple brings blessing to the surrounding land of promise (47:1–48:35).

---

12. These very blessings, along with the other new covenant blessings described by the prophets, were experienced by believers who lived prior to the new covenant. What distinguishes them as *new covenant* blessings is that now people from all nations experience them in comparative fullness.

In the second section describing the eschatological worship of the temple, God indicates that the sabbaths, once profaned by Israel, will be part of the renewed worship of God's people. When God details the job description of the priests, he indicates that "they shall keep my laws and my statutes in all my appointed feasts, and they shall keep my Sabbaths holy" (44:24). The priests who once "disregarded [God's] Sabbaths" so as to "profane" God (22:26) will now observe them and "keep [them] holy" (44:24). Thus, God's creational purposes for the Sabbath, once threatened by the sin of Israel's priests and of the nation of Israel as a whole, will come to realization in the eschatological worship that God will establish.[13]

Israel's eschatological "prince" will also play a critical role in leading Israel to observe God's sabbaths. God details his duties to include

> furnish[ing] the burnt offerings, grain offerings, and drink offerings, *at the feasts, the new moons, and the Sabbaths, all the appointed feasts of the house of Israel*: he shall provide the sin offerings, grain offerings, burnt offerings, and peace offerings, to make atonement on behalf of the house of Israel. (45:17)

The prince, then, plays an ancillary and supporting role to the priests in Israel's worship. He will provide the various offerings that God will require of his people, and he will see that they are provided at the appointed times. He will be faithful to ensure that God receives his due on "the Sabbaths" of the eschatological calendar of the worship of God. No less than the priests, the prince will be zealous for God's sabbaths.

Thus far, Ezekiel has shown the roles of priests and prince with respect to the various sabbaths of the worship of the eschatological

---

13. Hasel, "Sabbath," 852.

temple. The plurality of the sabbaths matches what is stipulated by the Pentateuch. But the weekly Sabbath retains its distinctiveness in this eschatological calendar. God commands that the "gate of the inner court that faces east shall be shut on the six working days, but on the Sabbath day it shall be opened, and on the day of the new moon it shall be opened" (46:1). On the Sabbath day, the prince goes before the people as far as the "vestibule of the gate," observing the priests making their offerings in the temple proper, offerings that the prince himself has supplied (46:2; cf. 46:4–5). The whole community, then, engages in Sabbath day worship, with prince, priests, and people each undertaking the roles that God has assigned to them.

Wonderfully, the New Testament tells us that these promises have found inaugurated fulfillment in the person and work of Christ. He is the Davidic prince whom God has raised up to shepherd the flock of God. With the Father, he has poured out the Spirit in fullness upon all nations, giving sinners new hearts and causing them to walk in God's laws. He is the eschatological temple, the heavenly high priest, and the once-for-all sacrificial offering by which sinners are brought near to God, on the basis of which we have been forgiven of all our sins and by which we have been sanctified. We are not waiting for Ezekiel 40–48 to take place at some point in our future—these events have already found their inaugurated fulfillment in Christ. The new covenant community has already begun to participate in the worship that Ezekiel describes for us in these chapters. That means that we expect the weekly Sabbath to factor, in some fashion, into the worship of the new covenant community. We will need to turn to the New Testament to get a concrete sense of what the Sabbath looks like in the age of inaugurated fulfillment. But before we turn to the pages of the New Testament, we need to explore one final testimony to the Sabbath in the Old Testament.

Nehemiah

Unlike Isaiah, Jeremiah, and Ezekiel, Nehemiah was neither a prophet nor a priest. Rather, he was a godly governor, sent by the Persian king to Jerusalem to rebuild the city's walls. Serving in the mid-fifth century BC, Nehemiah offers one of the last accounts in the Old Testament of Israel who is now restored to the land after exile, albeit under the rule of a foreign power.

In particular, Nehemiah gives us a snapshot of the spiritual well-being of the restoration community; he is concerned not only with rebuilding the physical boundaries around Jerusalem but also with establishing spiritual boundaries between God's people and the sur-rounding nations. If anything, he makes clear that the promised restoration of God's people, outlined in the canonical prophets, remains largely in their future. Yet, they must look to and work toward that future now.

To that end, during Nehemiah's tenure as governor, the people confessed their sins and made "a firm covenant in writing" (Neh. 9:38). In this covenant, the people "enter into a curse and an oath to walk in God's Law that was given by Moses the servant of God, and to observe and do all the commandments of the Lord our Lord and his rules and his statutes" (10:29). In particular, they agree that "if the peoples of the land bring in goods or any grain on the Sabbath day to sell, we will not buy from them on the Sabbath or on a holy day. And we will forego the crops of the seventh year and the exaction of every debt" (10:31). Positively, they agree to pay an annual tax for the upkeep of the temple and its worship, including "the Sabbaths" (10:32–33).

Thus, the people agree to commit themselves to Sabbath obser-vance. Knowing God's displeasure for conducting commerce on the Sabbath (see Jer. 17:19–27), they covenant to refrain from such activity. They furthermore commit their finances to support the worship of God on, among other occasions, his Sabbaths.

But this covenanted commitment soon falters. In the final chapter of the book, Nehemiah discovers that Israel has engaged in or permitted a number of shocking behaviors. In particular, they have performed work and engaged in commerce with resident aliens on the Sabbath (Neh. 13:15–16). Thus, Nehemiah confronts the leadership of the city, crying out, "What is this evil thing that you are doing, profaning the Sabbath day? Did not your fathers act in this way, and did not our God bring all this disaster on us and on this city? Now you are bringing more wrath on Israel by profaning the Sabbath" (13:17–18). In "profaning the Sabbath day," Nehemiah's generation has replicated the sins of their ancestors. They have failed to appreciate the judgment and "wrath" that such a sin invites. Because of this, Nehemiah takes steps to safeguard the Sabbath—he physically prevents the entry of goods to Jerusalem on the Sabbath and keeps non-Jewish merchants at a distance from the city walls on the Sabbath (13:19–21). Further, he enlists the Levites to "purify themselves and come and guard the gates, to keep the Sabbath day holy" (13:22).

Overall, this scene, coupled with the covenant documented in Nehemiah 10, is a grim one. Nehemiah must resort to restraints and force to ensure that the Sabbath is observed in Jerusalem. But these "external measures were inadequate, in the last resort, to control the perversities of the human heart," a state of affairs that only underscores the as-yet-unrealized fulfillment of the Old Testament's prophecies of spiritual restoration.[14] Thus, the book leaves us with "a sense of anticlimax."[15] The restoration of the sixth and fifth centuries BC is manifestly not that fulfillment. As the curtain closes upon the Old Testament, that hope remains in the future. And the longing for that hope propels us into the pages of the New Testament.

---

14. H. G. M. Williamson, *Ezra-Nehemiah*, Word Biblical Commentary 16 (Waco, TX: Word Books, 1985), 402.

15. Williamson, *Ezra-Nehemiah*, 402.

Conclusions

In sum, the prophets of the Old Testament set before us two primary realities. The first is that both kingdoms, Israel and Judah, violated their covenant charter with God. They did so by disobeying God's laws and by stubbornly resisting the prophets' calls to repentance. In particular, they displeased God by violating his sabbaths, the appointed sign of the Mosaic covenant. Both the people and the priests were culpable for profaning God's sabbaths and refusing to worship him in the way that he had commanded in his law. Although not a prophet, Nehemiah shows us that the restoration of Israel to the land did not effect a fundamental change of heart within Israel toward God's law and, in particular, his Sabbath.

The second reality is the restoration that God promises his people. Isaiah shows us that God will restore true worship that comes from the heart. Further, this worship will be offered by people drawn from the whole range of humanity—Jew, foreigner, and eunuch. God will gather them to his holy mountain by his saving power. The creational purposes for the Sabbath—blessing in the worship of the holy God—will come to realization in the lives of men and women. Thus, the blessing that Jeremiah told his contemporaries could have been theirs is the blessing that God will eventually bring to pass in the lives of his people. Ezekiel clearly shows God's intention to bring about a new shepherd-prince, a new covenant, and a new temple. And the Sabbath will be the occasion when prince, priest, and people will gather in the presence of God to worship him and to experience the blessing of his sanctifying presence.

Ultimately, these prophetic realities find their fulfillment in Christ. The New Testament shows us how God will bring his purposes for humanity—first announced at creation and subsequently developed in the Law and the Prophets—to their intended realization in the last Adam, Jesus Christ. Thus, in the next chapter, we will explore the Gospels' testimony to the earthly ministry of Christ and, particularly, how the arrival of Christ signaled the beginnings of what God had long ago promised in the prophets.

4

Christ

When we turn in the New Testament to the Gospels, we see that the Sabbath was very much part of the life and ministry of Jesus Christ. In this chapter, we are going to explore what Jesus had to say about the Sabbath and what he did on the Sabbath. Overall, his words and deeds help us to see God's true intention for the Sabbath and the way in which we ought to understand it in light of the person and work of Christ.

Redemptive History and the Public Ministry of Christ

Before we look at the passages in the Gospels that show us what Christ both said about the Sabbath and did on the Sabbath, we need to step back and think about the place of his ministry within redemptive history. Because the Gospels appear in the New Testament alongside Acts, the Epistles, and Revelation, it is tempting to group all these books together. But, in an important way, the Gospels stand apart from the rest of the New Testament. Acts, the Epistles, and Revelation all describe events that take place after the resurrection of Christ. While the Gospels were written after the resurrection and from a postresurrection perspective, they describe events that, for the most part, took place before the resurrection.

At first glance, this might seem to be a pedantic point. But it is significant for our understanding of the shape and flow of redemptive history, and it is particularly important for the way that we read the New Testament's testimony about the Sabbath. In our first chapter, we saw from 1 Corinthians 15 how Paul understands human history in terms of the person and work of two representative men, Adam and "the last Adam" (1 Cor. 15:45). Adam sinned against God and so failed to realize God's purposes for humanity. But the last Adam has brought those purposes to their intended fulfillment and did so when he was raised gloriously from the dead. Although the people of God have yet to experience the fullness of what Christ accomplished in his resurrection, we have already been introduced into the new creation and now share in his resurrection life (see 2 Cor. 5:17).[1]

The resurrection of Christ, then, is the beginning of the fulfillment of God's purposes for creation. It marks a bright dividing line in redemptive history. In particular, the resurrection marks the formal beginning of the new covenant. This means that the period of history documented in the Gospels prior to the resurrection falls properly under the Mosaic covenant; thus, the ministry of Jesus takes us to the close of the Mosaic covenant even as it prepares us for the dawn of the new covenant. For this reason, we will look in this chapter at what the Gospels tell us about the Sabbath prior to Jesus's resurrection and, in the next chapter, at the New Testament's testimony to the Sabbath both at and after his resurrection.

But before we turn to the testimony of the Gospels regarding the Sabbath in general, we will look briefly at several passages that

---

1. Before the resurrection, sinners were saved on the same basis as sinners after the resurrection—the merits of Christ alone. They were saved through faith in the Messiah who was yet to come; we are saved through faith in the Messiah who has already come.

confirm that the public ministry as well as the death and burial of Jesus took place during and under the Mosaic covenant. First, Luke tells us that Jesus inaugurated his public ministry at "the synagogue" in Nazareth "on the Sabbath day" (Luke 4:16). He read a portion of the prophet Isaiah and then declared that this prophecy had found its fulfillment in himself (4:18–19, 21). We will look at what Jesus said about that particular Scripture in the next section, but for now we may note the importance of the occasion of the beginning of Jesus's public ministry, namely, the Sabbath. As the Gospels go on to tell us, Jesus regularly attended the worship of God's people in local synagogues on the Sabbath (see 4:44; 13:1–10). As his parents had been faithful to raise him in obedience to the demands of the Mosaic law (see 2:22–52), so Jesus was himself faithful to observe this law. This observance included the regular keeping of the Sabbath. And, as John's Gospel tells us, it also included the regular observance of the annual festivals, including Passover (John 2, 5, 6, 12) and Tabernacles (John 7–8).

Second, one of Jesus's first miracles, according to Mark's Gospel, was the cleansing of a leper (Mark 1:40–45). When Jesus cleanses him, he tells the man, "See that you say nothing to anyone, but go, show yourself to the priest and offer for your cleansing what Moses commanded, for a proof to them" (1:44). The legal background to Jesus's words is Leviticus 14:1–32, where God gives Israel, through Moses, directions to the priests regarding people who had been cleansed of leprosy. Thus Jesus, knowing that this man has been truly cleansed, commands the man to present to the priest the offering that the Mosaic law required of a cleansed man. This offering, Jesus says, will be "a proof to them." Among other things, this offering shows that Jesus's ministry was undertaken under the Mosaic covenant and in such a way as to honor the Mosaic law. In fact, it would be along these lines that he would bring the law to fulfillment (see Matt. 5:17).

Third, in an incident that only Matthew records, officials came to Capernaum to collect the "two-drachma tax," a tax that God had required of every Israelite under the law (Matt. 17:24; see Ex. 30:16). The tax collectors ask Peter whether Jesus will pay the tax, and Peter responds "yes" (Matt. 17:24–25). Then, when Peter and Jesus are next together, Jesus asks Peter, "From whom do kings of the earth take toll or tax? From their sons or from others?" (17:25). Peter answers, "From others," and Jesus declares, "Then the sons are free" (17:26). Here, Jesus is asserting his right of exemption from the census tax. This right belongs to him as "son" of the "king." As the Son of God, Jesus is in a different category than every other Israelite. Even so, he says to Peter, so as to not "give offense to them, go to the sea and cast a hook and take the first fish that comes up, and when you open its mouth you will find a shekel. Take that and give it to them for me and for yourself" (17:27). Thus, in the interests of not giving "offense," Jesus will pay the tax. But the manner in which Peter retrieves the money to pay the tax for both of them simply confirms the point—Jesus is unlike any other Israelite and is in unique relationship with God as his Son. Jesus, to be sure, kept the Mosaic law for the duration of his life and ministry. Yet he did so as one who, by right, was not bound to its demands—he willingly submitted himself to its requirements in order to accomplish his saving mission on earth.

Fourth, at the end of his public ministry, Jesus pronounced a series of "woes" against the scribes and the Pharisees (Matt. 23:1–36). Before he utters his first "woe," Jesus says something surprising to the "crowds" and "disciples" (23:1)—"the scribes and the Pharisees sit on Moses' seat, so do and observe whatever they tell you, but not the works they do. For they preach but do not practice" (23:2–3). When Jesus says that the scribes and Pharisees sit on "Moses' seat," he is recognizing their legitimate teaching authority. He tells his disciples to "do and observe whatever they tell you." However, here and elsewhere in the Gospels, Jesus corrects the teaching of these groups, even accusing them of nullifying the word of God for the sake of their traditions (see 15:1–9). Jesus, then, affirms that people are to follow the teaching of the scribes and Pharisees insofar as those teachings conform to what God has already said in the Bible. Yet, he criticizes the way that their "practice" diverges from their teaching (23:3), such as when they lay crushing burdens on people but refuse to help them to bear those burdens (23:4).

Jesus's recognition of the legitimacy of the scribes and Pharisees as teachers among God's people is critical to bear in mind, especially in light of the "woes" that follow. He exposes the departures of what these learned men teach from the Scripture, and he exposes their hypocrisy, that is, the disjunction between what they say and how they live. But, for all these failings, he never faults them for teaching the law of Moses. They are right to teach God's people the laws of the Mosaic covenant; the problems come when they depart from those laws or try to add to those laws. Overall, Jesus's approach toward these teachers confirms that he was consciously conducting his earthly ministry under the Mosaic covenant.

There is a pattern, then, across Jesus's earthly ministry of his willing observance of the requirements of the Mosaic covenant. He habitually worshipped in the synagogue on the Sabbath day, and he traveled to Jerusalem for the annual festivals required by the Mosaic law. He upheld and honored the laws of purification and the census tax. He affirmed the faithful teaching of the laws of the Mosaic covenant, even as he decried those who added human requirements to those laws. Thus, Jesus's earthly ministry took place under the Mosaic covenant, but he did not do these things by necessity of nature. He was and is, after all, the God-man. So he followed the Mosaic law *voluntarily*, in order to carry out his mediatorial mission to save sinners by obeying the law of God on their behalf, and, ultimately, to bear its curse on their behalf.

Broadly speaking, the Gospels point to the death and burial of Jesus as the conclusion of the era of the Mosaic covenant and to the resurrection of Jesus as the historical beginning of the new covenant. We will look at what the Gospels say about the resurrection in the next chapter. For the moment, we may simply look at the accounts of Jesus's death and burial.

Jesus died on a Friday afternoon, just hours before the start of the Jewish Sabbath at sunset. In haste, Joseph of Arimathea arranged for Jesus's body to be removed from the cross and placed in a fresh, new tomb near the site of the cross (Matt. 27:57–61). Mark makes a point of saying that Jesus was buried *before* the Sabbath officially started (Mark 15:42). Further, Luke stresses that even though "the women who had come with [Jesus] from Galilee" had "prepared spices and ointments," they did not immediately go to apply those spices and ointments to the body of Jesus because "on the Sabbath they rested according to the commandment" (Luke 23:55–56). Thus, Jesus's disciples exhibit a pattern of concluding their work (including the burial of Jesus and all the details surrounding it) before the Sabbath began on Friday night and of resting on the Sabbath day (Friday night through Saturday evening).

Yet, Matthew tells us of some extraordinary events that took place while Jesus was on the cross and had profound implications for the Mosaic law. Matthew 27:51–54 reads:

> And behold, the curtain of the temple was torn in two, from top to bottom. And the earth shook, and the rocks were split. The tombs also were opened. And many bodies of the saints who had fallen asleep were raised, and coming out of the tombs after his resurrection they went into the holy city and

appeared to many. When the centurion and those who were with him, keeping watch over Jesus, saw the earthquake and what took place, they were filled with awe and said, "Truly this was the Son of God!"

Two points about this passage are worth noting. First, the temple curtain, the curtain dividing the Holy of Holies from the Holy Place, is "torn in two, from top to bottom" (Matt. 27:51). This tearing is manifestly supernatural, the immediate work of God. It signals that at the death of Christ, the temple, with its sacrifices, priests, and cleansings, had been brought to an official end in the history of redemption.[2]

Second, "the earth shook, and the rocks were split. The tombs also were opened" (27:51–52). This shaking and rending of the earth and the resurrection of the dead are indicators, according to Old Testament prophecy, of the Day of the Lord (see Ps. 97:5; Isa. 13:13; Dan. 12:2–3; Nah. 1:5; Hag. 2:6–7). Thus, conjoined with the conclusion of the Mosaic covenant is the eschatological presence of God that signaled the arrival of something new. To be sure, the phenomena that Matthew describes were local and temporary. The earthquake and the resurrection took place in and around Jerusalem, and the saints who were raised from the dead went on to die (again) at a later time. The death of Jesus, then, does not herald the absolute end of history.

But his death does mark the end of the old order and the dawn of something brand new. Matthew gives us a hint of new things to come when he documents the Gentile centurion confessing Jesus to be the Son of God (Matt. 27:54). Soon, the gospel of Christ will go

---

2. The temple, of course, would continue to stand until the Romans effectively destroyed it in AD 70. But God is announcing in this miraculous event that the temple had served its purpose in redemptive history and that, from this point forward, sinners would approach him immediately through the finished work of the heavenly high priest, Jesus Christ.

to all the nations, both Jew and Gentile will together confess Christ as Savior and Lord, and Christ will be present with his people by the Holy Spirit (see 28:18–20).

Overall, this survey of Jesus's earthly ministry in redemptive-historical context sets the stage for our study of what Jesus had to say about the Sabbath and what he did on the Sabbath. Our expectation is that Jesus will fully uphold the Mosaic Sabbath. But, in light of what he says about the teaching of the scribes and Pharisees (23:1–36), we anticipate that he will correct errors that have crept up surrounding the Old Testament's teaching of the Sabbath. Further, because Jesus has come on a mission to save sinners and, in this way, to usher into history the age to come and the new creation, we will look for Jesus to identify ways in which the Sabbath has its full meaning in relation to his person and work.

Jesus and the Sabbath: The Synoptic Gospels

We may now turn to the testimony of Jesus and the Sabbath in the Gospels. First, we will look at the Synoptic Gospels (Matthew, Mark, and Luke). Then, we will look at what John's Gospel has to say.

There are seven primary passages in the Synoptic Gospels that speak of Jesus in relation to the Sabbath, and we may group these passages into three overlapping categories. The second two relate to the miracles that Jesus performed and his debates with Jewish leadership. The first is a category all unto itself—Jesus's inaugural sermon in Luke 4:16–30.

1. LUKE 4:16–30

Earlier, we saw the significance of Jesus giving his inaugural sermon in a synagogue service on the Sabbath (Luke 4:16–30). Now we may return to this passage and explore what Jesus told this congregation in Nazareth on that occasion. The passage that he selected, Isaiah

61:1 and 2, contains images and themes that express the emphases of the ministry Jesus is about to undertake. They also happen to touch upon some of the main lines of the Old Testament's teaching about the Sabbath.

Jesus first identifies himself as one "anointed" by the "Spirit of the Lord" to "proclaim good news to the poor" (Luke 4:18). The ministry of God's Messiah ("Anointed One") will be to preach—specifically, he will preach a message of "good news" to those who are "poor." In the Old Testament, the "poor" are those people within the covenant community who, oppressed by their enemies, look to God for vindication and relief: "In contrast to those who have fastened their hope upon this world, [the poor] expect the salvation God has held out to his people as 'the consolation of Israel.'"[3] Thus, Jesus here announces that he has come to proclaim that longed-for salvation.

Overall, his quotation of Isaiah describes this salvation in a couple of important ways. He has come to proclaim the "recovering of sight to the blind" (Luke 4:18), "proclaim liberty to the captives," and "set at liberty those who are oppressed, to proclaim the year of the Lord's favor" (4:18, 19). The background to "the year of the Lord's favor" is Leviticus 25:10, where God had commanded regarding the year of jubilee, "you shall . . . proclaim liberty throughout the land to all its inhabitants." Thus Jesus is saying that what the year of jubilee anticipated ("liberty") is what he has come to "proclaim" and accomplish. He confirms this point after reading from the scroll, when, in verse 21, he declares, "Today this Scripture has been fulfilled in your hearing."

Strikingly, Jesus claims that the year of jubilee is fulfilled in his person and work as Israel's Messiah. The year of jubilee is the apex of the calendrical pyramid that God gives his people in Leviticus. Observed every fiftieth year, it sits atop the weekly Sabbaths and the seventh-year

---

3. Herman Ridderbos, *The Coming of the Kingdom*, trans. H. de Jongste (Phillipsburg, NJ: P&R, 1962), 189.

Sabbath.[4] As such—and Jesus will go on to confirm this point later in his public ministry—the whole of the Old Testament calendar, including the weekly Sabbath, points to and finds its fulfillment in Christ.[5]

Thus, although Jesus does not explicitly mention the Sabbath in this inaugural sermon, the themes that he emphasizes from Isaiah's prophecy highlight what the Old Testament teaches about the significance of the Sabbath. In Deuteronomy, God tells Israel to remember each Sabbath how he had delivered them from slavery in Egypt (Deut. 5:15), and on this Sabbath in Nazareth, Jesus announces "liberty" to "the captives" and for "those who are oppressed" (Luke 4:18). Jesus does not merely herald this freedom but also says that he will be the one who frees the oppressed. In the Old Testament, the Sabbath looked back to the exodus, when God delivered his captive people from the hand of their oppressor. Now, Jesus Christ will undertake a new and greater exodus, in which he delivers sinners from sin by his death on the cross and by his subsequent resurrection from the dead. This is the point that Luke later makes in reporting Jesus's conversations with Moses and Elijah on the Mount of Transfiguration—"Moses and Elijah . . . appeared in glory and spoke of his departure [Greek *exodos*], which he was about to accomplish at Jerusalem" (9:30–31). Thus, the deliverance and the liberty that were part of the remembrance involved in Israel's weekly Sabbath observance are soon to find their intended realization in Jesus Christ. What the Sabbath had anticipated, Jesus Christ will soon accomplish.

2. MIRACLES

In general, Jesus's ministry was known for the performance of miracles, so much so that Peter could say to the household of Cornelius,

---

4. See my discussion of the year of jubilee in chapter 2.

5. This is a point, we shall see below, that John's Gospel is especially concerned to emphasize—the temple in Jerusalem and all its feasts and festivals find their intended fulfillment in the person and work of Christ.

"God anointed Jesus of Nazareth with the Holy Spirit and with power. He went about doing good and healing all who were oppressed by the devil, for God was with him" (Acts 10:38). Miracles, Peter says here, demonstrated that Christ had come to do "good." As such, they were three-dimensional portraits of the saving victory that he would accomplish in his death and resurrection as well as indicators of the abiding presence of God in his life and ministry.

Overall, Jesus's miracles were purposefully paired with his preaching ministry (see Matt. 4:23; 9:35). Although his preaching ministry had priority over his miracles (see Mark 1:35–39), his teaching and his works of power complemented one another. In his earthly ministry, miracles "make visible and audible the fulfillment of the promises, the coming of the great era of salvation . . . the coming of the kingdom of God."[6] In fact, Jesus's miracles display different aspects of the way in which he saves sinners from their sins and brings them eternal life. Thus, the variety of miracles that Jesus performed helps to highlight the many dimensions of the salvation that Christ came to accomplish and of the kingdom into which he brings his people. And since several of his miracles took place on the Sabbath, these miracles help us to see the meaning of his ministry in light of the Sabbath. In turn, his person and work lend insight into the meaning of the Sabbath. We will look now at five miracles that he performed on the Sabbath as each helps us to understand, in different ways, the true identity both of Jesus and this holy day.

First, Jesus meets "a man with an unclean spirit" in the synagogue at Capernaum on the Sabbath (Mark 1:23). The demons who possess this man call out to Jesus, "What have you to do with us, Jesus of Nazareth? Have you come to destroy us? I know who you are—the Holy One of God" (1:24). Although the demons who have taken

---

6. Ridderbos, *Coming of the Kingdom*, 65.

control of this man's life have no concern for his well-being, they are quite concerned for theirs. These unclean demons know that Jesus is "holy" and that he has come on a mission to conquer them. But that victory awaits the cross. For now, he commands them to silence and to "come out of" the man they possess (1:25). The demons comply immediately. As a result, those present at the synagogue cry out, "What is this? A new teaching with authority! He commands even the unclean spirits, and they obey him" (1:27). This reaction shows us that Jesus's exorcism confirms the "authority" of the "new teaching" of the arrival of the kingdom (see 1:14–15). It also points to what he has come to do—"to destroy the works of the devil" (1 John 3:8). It is therefore not incidental that Jesus performs this miracle on the Sabbath, the day when Israel was called to remember their redemption from bondage in Egypt—his exorcism points to the redemption that he would accomplish at the cross, a redemption shadowed by Israel's deliverance from bondage in Egypt.

Second, after this episode, Jesus "immediately" left the synagogue in Capernaum and "entered the house of Simon and Andrew, with James and John" (Mark 1:29). It was, therefore, still the Sabbath. Here, Jesus found Peter's "mother-in-law . . . ill with a fever" (1:30), so he "came and took her by the hand and lifted her up, and the fever left her" (1:31). Fever, like every disease and affliction, has entered the world because of sin.[7] Thus, in healing Peter's mother-in-law, Jesus shows that he has come into the world to roll back the curse that is the result of sin's entrance into the world (cf. Matt. 8:17).

Yet, just as Jesus takes away illness, he also restores to health. Thus, as a sign of such health, Peter's mother-in-law "began to serve them" (Mark 1:31). It is a mark of this woman's restoration that she

---

7. This is not to say that Peter's mother-in-law necessarily suffered from this fever as the punishment or result of some specific sin in her life. Jesus elsewhere teaches that we may not draw such conclusions from the fact of illness or disability in a person's life (see John 9:1–3).

devotes herself to the service of Jesus and his disciples. She does so from love to Jesus Christ. Overall, service of this kind is precisely what God intended for human beings at their creation, and Christ's work of redemption is the way in which God will bring his creation purposes for human beings to fruition.

As these passages show, the removal of sin from human beings and the realization of God's purposes for humanity at creation are both tied to the Old Testament's teaching about the Sabbath (the day when this healing takes place). The Sabbath is, on the one hand, the day when God's redeemed were to reflect in gratitude on what he had done to redeem them from bondage in Egypt; this exodus shadows the new exodus in Christ. On the other hand, the Sabbath is the day when human beings remember the highest end of our created existence—the worship of God. Thus, overall, Jesus is creating a community of redeemed sinners who are characterized by the service of others and by their devotion to and worship of him.[8]

Third, we may briefly look at three passages (which we will explore in more detail in the next section) where Jesus performs a distinct healing in the synagogue on the Sabbath day. In Mark 3:1–6, Jesus heals a man with a "withered hand" on the Sabbath (Mark 3:1) and defends his action by stating that it is "lawful on the Sabbath to do good, . . . to save life" (3:4). Similarly, in Luke 13:10–17, Jesus heals a woman who "had had a disabling spirit for eighteen years" (Luke 13:11). She is not possessed by a demon, but it appears that a demon had afflicted her physically for a long time. Jesus heals her, declaring, "Woman, you are freed from your disability" (13:12). He then

---

8. Samuele Bacchiocchi, noting Luke's order of Jesus's inaugural sermon followed by the two miracles of the exorcism of demons from the man in the synagogue and of the healing of Peter's mother-in-law (Luke 4:16–21, 31–37, 38–39), observes how these three accounts highlight "the meaning of the Sabbath as *redemption, joy* and *service*," a meaning "revealed more explicitly in the subsequent Sabbath ministry of Christ." Samuele Bacchiocchi, *From Sabbath to Sunday: A Historical Investigation of the Rise of Sunday Observance in Early Christianity* (Rome: Pontifical Gregorian University Press, 1977), 30; italics in the original.

defends himself against his critics, arguing that his freeing of this woman from her disability is a fitting thing to do "on the Sabbath day" (13:16). Last, in Luke 14:1–6, Jesus heals a man of dropsy on the Sabbath. Against the implied criticism of those who are present on that occasion, Jesus again argues that it is "lawful to heal on the Sabbath" (14:3) and that what he has done is no different than rescuing "a son or an ox" who had "fallen into a well on a Sabbath day" (14:5).

In each of these three accounts, Jesus performs a restorative miracle of healing on the Sabbath day—a withered hand is made whole; a woman afflicted with a disabling spirit is freed; a man with dropsy is healed. In each case, a human being suffers some ailment or affliction that is a consequence of humanity's fall into sin. In each case, Jesus makes the healing a teaching moment. The Sabbath is a day to "save life" (Mark 3:4), to free a woman in bondage (Luke 13:12), to "heal" a man who is as helpless in his disease as an animal or a person trapped in a well (Luke 14:3). Thus, Jesus connects his ministry of saving sinners to the Sabbath as a day of spiritual life, health, and freedom. Because of sin, human beings are unable to enter into the Sabbath rest that God established at the creation for humanity; but Jesus Christ has come to bring his people into the experience and enjoyment of that rest.

3. CONTROVERSIES

As we have already begun to see, the Sabbath was an occasion for controversy between Jesus and the religious leadership of his day. In each case, it is the Jewish teachers who accuse Jesus of violating the Sabbath. In response, Jesus not only clears himself of the charge but also highlights the true meaning and purpose of the Sabbath in the course of his self-vindication. There are four such passages in the Synoptic Gospels.

The first appears at the beginning of Jesus's ministry, as Mark records it (Mark 2:23–28). Here, Jesus and his disciples are "going through the grainfields" on the Sabbath (2:23). As they do so, "his disciples beg[i]n to pluck heads of grain" (2:23). When the Pharisees hear of this, they accuse the disciples of "doing what is not lawful on the Sabbath"—as they deem the plucking of heads of grain to be the kind of work forbidden on this day—and thus implicitly accuse Jesus of permitting that allegedly sinful activity (2:24).[9]

Overall, it is telling that Jesus neither here nor on any other occasion in his earthly ministry concedes the Pharisees' point—that is to say, he does not agree that what his disciples are doing is work forbidden by the law of God. On the contrary, Jesus proceeds first to defend his disciples' actions and then to affirm his right to declare what is proper activity on the Sabbath.

First, he defends his disciples' actions, citing the example of David arriving at Nob to Ahimelech the priest (2:25–26; see 1 Sam. 21:1–6).[10] Here, David was fleeing for his life from Saul, and he and his men were hungry. Then, David received from the high priest "the bread of the Presence, which it is not lawful for any but the priests to eat," and proceeded to eat it with his men (Mark 2:26). So what is Jesus's point? Ordinarily, he says, only the priests may eat the bread of the Presence. But a situation arose in which the lives of David and his men depended upon eating that bread. When they ate it, God did not disapprove of their eating. Thus, Jesus's point is that God's law

---

9. In Deuteronomy 23:25, God permits travelers in Israel to do precisely what the disciples did. The Pharisees do not accuse them of theft, however, but of performing what they deem to be work on the Sabbath day.

10. Mark's text reads "Abiathar," and 1 Samuel reads "Ahimelech." Abiathar was the son of Ahimelech and the lone survivor of the massacre at Nob, undertaken, on Saul's orders, by Doeg the Edomite (1 Sam. 22:6–19). Abiathar likely served alongside his father in the incident of 1 Samuel 21 and certainly succeeded his father after his father's murder. Those facts help to account for Jesus speaking of the incident of 1 Samuel 21:1–6 "in the time of Abiathar" (Mark 2:26; see the note on Mark 2:25–26 in Hans F. Bayer, study notes in *ESV Study Bible*, ed. Wayne Grudem [Wheaton, IL: Crossway, 2008], 1897).

was never designed to crush or destroy human beings. This is what he means when he says in the next verse, "The Sabbath was made for man, not man for the Sabbath" (2:27). And, if the principle that the law is given for the benefit of human beings and not their destruction applies to the laws governing the eating of the bread of the Presence, then it applies to each one of God's laws, including the Sabbath law.[11] Jesus could simply have said, "God never forbade this kind of activity on the Sabbath day." And he does say that, but he takes it one step further because he wants his opponents to understand how they have misunderstood God's purposes and intentions in giving humanity the Sabbath.

In Matthew's account, after he gives the illustration of David eating the bread of the Presence, Jesus goes on to say, "have you not read in the Law how on the Sabbath the priests in the temple profane the Sabbath and are guiltless? I tell you, something greater than the temple is here" (Matt. 12:5–6). Here, Jesus uses shocking language ("the priests in the temple profane the Sabbath") to make a point. If the Pharisees were consistent with their own principle, they would have to declare the priests to be violating the Sabbath just as much as Jesus's disciples.[12] But the kind of activity the priests undertook on the Sabbath was not displeasing to God. Rather, it was pleasing to him. Neither the temple priests nor Jesus's disciples were violating the Sabbath. Each was engaged in activity that was acceptable to God on that day.

Following this second argument, Jesus begins to bring his response to the Pharisees to a close by highlighting his authority with respect to the Sabbath. He first tells them that "something greater than the temple is here" (12:6). It is precisely because Jesus

---

11. See a similar interpretation in Matthew Poole, *Commentary on the Holy Bible, Volume III: Matthew to Revelation* (Peabody, MA: Hendrickson, n.d.), 52.

12. Poole, *Commentary*, 53.

is greater than the temple that he has the authority to pronounce the activity of his disciples on the Sabbath to be lawful. The sense in which Jesus is "greater than the temple" is addressed two verses later, when he says that the "Son of Man is lord of the Sabbath" (12:8; Mark 2:28). Thus, Jesus asserts authority not only over the temple but also over the Sabbath. In fact, it is as he is the "Son of Man" that he is "lord of the Sabbath." The title "Son of Man" is one of Jesus's favorites and has roots in the Old Testament. In particular, Jesus's use of the term reflects what the prophet Daniel had written centuries before:

> I saw in the night visions, and behold, with the clouds of heaven there came one like a son of man, and he came to the Ancient of Days and was presented before him. And to him was given dominion and glory and a kingdom, that all peoples, nations, and languages should serve him; his dominion is an everlasting dominion, which shall not pass away, and his kingdom one that shall not be destroyed. (Dan. 7:13–14)

Jesus says, then, that his lordship, described in this prophetic vision, encompasses the Sabbath.[13] It is as he is the Messiah, whose kingdom encompasses peoples of all nations, that he authoritatively declares what is and is not proper to do on the Sabbath. But Jesus's claim of authority reaches higher still. In claiming to be "lord of the Sabbath," he is asserting authority over a commandment of God. It is difficult to escape the conclusion that Jesus is making a claim to deity here; after all, only God the lawgiver has such authority over any of the commands of the law that he gives to human beings.

In light of this Messianic and divine authority, Matthew's and Mark's accounts close with two positive and complementary

---

13. B. B. Warfield, "The Sabbath," 310.

statements regarding the Sabbath activity that God approves.[14] First, in Mark 2:27, Jesus says, "the Sabbath was made for man, not man for the Sabbath." This statement, we saw in an earlier chapter, points to the Sabbath as an ordinance of the creation. It pertains to all human beings. Jesus can make this claim because he is both Messiah and God, as he says in the next verse, "So the Son of Man is lord even of the Sabbath" (Mark 2:28). He reiterates that God has intended the Sabbath for the benefit and well-being of human beings; it is not designed to harm, suppress, or crush our God-given humanity. Thus Jesus, far from joining in the Pharisees' censure of his disciples, affirms his disciples when they gather food to eat as they go about his business on the Sabbath day.

Second, in Matthew 12:7, Jesus, quoting the prophet Hosea, says, "And if you had known what this means, 'I desire mercy, and not sacrifice,' you would not have condemned the guiltless" (cf. Matt. 9:13). Here Jesus is not commenting on the law of God so much as on the Pharisees as interpreters of the law of God. As Herman N. Ridderbos explains, "The Pharisees' concentration on the external forms of religion made them blind toward the true purpose and meaning of the law: love for God and one's neighbor."[15] In other words, their readiness to condemn the disciples is symptomatic of a deeper failure to grasp what the law of God is really about. Thus, this controversy is not a matter of refined and nuanced differing interpretations of a portion of God's law—it is a matter of two altogether radically different conceptions of God's law.

The remaining three passages addressing Jewish leaders' opposition to Jesus concerning the Sabbath are passages that we explored

---

14. Note that the statement about Sabbath observance in Mark 2:27 finds its ground in Jesus's claim to authority in Mark 2:28. Similarly, the statement about Sabbath observance in Matthew 12:7 finds its ground in Matthew 12:8.

15. Herman N. Ridderbos, *Matthew*, trans. Ray Togtman, Bible Student's Commentary (Grand Rapids: Zondervan, 1987), 230.

briefly above—Jesus's healing of a man with the withered hand (Mark 3:1–6), Jesus's healing of a woman with a disabling spirit (Luke 13:1–7), and Jesus's healing of a man with dropsy (14:1–6). Now, we may see what Jesus has to say about the Sabbath in light of his opponents' criticisms of his activities on the Sabbath.

First, Jesus invites a man with a withered hand to step forward in the synagogue (Mark 3:3). He then asks the Pharisees, "Is it lawful on the Sabbath to do good or to do harm, to save life or to kill?" (3:4). The very form of the question shows that Jesus understands the Sabbath to be a day when it is lawful to "do good" and to "save life." Thus, the Pharisees' refusal to answer his question betrays their "hardness of heart" (3:5). And when Jesus heals the man, the Pharisees further demonstrate this hardness of heart by conspiring "with the Herodians against him, how to destroy him" (3:6).

Second, when Jesus heals the woman with the disabling spirit, the "ruler of the synagogue" is "indignant because Jesus had healed on the Sabbath" (Luke 13:14). He turns not to Jesus but to the people and instructs them to seek healing on the other six days of the week, since those are the days "in which work ought to be done" (13:14). Having been baldly accused of violating the letter of the Sabbath command, Jesus in turn accuses his opponents of hypocrisy—they would have no objection to "unty[ing]" their oxen and donkeys to bring them to water (13:15), but they would forbid a suffering "daughter of Abraham" from being "loosed from [her] bond on the Sabbath day" (13:16).

Third, in the case of the man with dropsy, Jesus asks the Pharisees the question, "Is it lawful to heal on the Sabbath, or not?" (14:3) and is met with silence (14:4). After Jesus heals the man, he asks them whether they would not rescue an ox or a son who had fallen into a well on the Sabbath. Jesus's reasoning is clear—if they would deliver cattle or human beings from such distress on the Sabbath, how could they deny this man the opportunity to be healed of his infirmity on the Sabbath?

Overall, in each of these three passages, Jesus confirms the radically different approaches to the law of God that we observed above in his confrontations with the Jewish leadership about the Sabbath. His opponents legislate the prohibitions on work so expansively that they transform the Sabbath into a crushing load upon the backs of human beings. They would prefer to leave people in their suffering and misery than to allow Jesus to relieve them. Jesus, however, stresses that his opponents do not truly understand the Sabbath commandment. By implication, he declares that their rules have no warrant in the law of God and, in fact, contradict both the spirit and the letter of the Sabbath command. Thus, far from abolishing or weakening the Sabbath command, Jesus is attempting to restore the rightful meaning and observance of the Sabbath among a people whose leaders have fundamentally corrupted it.

Jesus and the Sabbath: The Gospel according to John

In John's Gospel, Jesus makes claims about the Sabbath that complement the reports of his teaching and activity on the Sabbath in the Synoptic Gospels. We may first look at how John generally shows us Jesus's relationship to Israel's worship before we explore the Sabbath in particular. Overall, in John, Jesus also presents himself as the one in whom the Jerusalem temple finds its fulfillment (John 2:13–22; cf. Matt. 12:6).[16] By making this claim, he pinpoints his resurrection from the dead as the moment at which the Jerusalem temple will have arrived at its divinely appointed end in redemptive history. After the resurrection, the temple will be found in the risen Christ

---

16. The material that follows in this paragraph has been drawn from my book, *The Lord's Supper as the Sign and Meal of the New Covenant*, Short Studies in Biblical Theology (Wheaton, IL: Crossway, 2019), 78–79.

and in his body, the church (see Eph. 2:11–22). Further, John shows us that all of the festivals in the Old Testament also find their fulfillment in Christ. In this Gospel, Jesus is present at such various major Old Testament festivals as Tabernacles (John 7–8) and Passover (John 2; 5; 6; 12–19), and at each we see the ways in which those festivals distinctly pointed to him and how he represents their intended and ultimate fulfillment. For example, in his conversation with the Samaritan woman, Jesus points to an epochal transformation in the worship of God's people in light of his death and resurrection (see 4:21–24). Therefore, these festivals will not continue to be observed by God's people in the age of eschatological fulfillment inaugurated by Jesus's resurrection; neither they nor the Jerusalem temple will carry over into this eschatological worship.

When Jesus teaches about the Sabbath in John's Gospel, however, he makes clear that the Sabbath continues into the age of eschatological fulfillment. The Sabbath surfaces in his public teaching on at least three occasions. First, in John 5:1–18, he is accused of breaking the Sabbath because he healed a paralyzed man on that day (John 5:16, 18). Jesus defends his actions by telling his critics, "My Father is working until now, and I am working" (5:17). But this defense enrages the Jewish leadership who then "were seeking all the more to kill him, because not only was he breaking the Sabbath, but he was even calling God his own Father, making himself equal with God" (5:18).

Here, Jesus makes two important claims in the course of this defense. First, he asserts equality with God, a matter that Jesus further addresses in the remainder of the chapter (5:19–47). Second, he does not concede his opponents' claim that he was violating the Sabbath. On the contrary, he defends his activity as appropriate to the Sabbath. God had made the world in six days and rested the seventh day. But, Jesus observes, the Father is "working until now." This means that "all the while the Sabbath command was in force, God was in fact working. In other words, the Sabbath command does not mean doing nothing but doing the work of God."[17] Thus, in healing the paralytic, Jesus is doing work that is appropriate to the Sabbath day. And in making this assertion, he thereby places himself in the same category as his heavenly Father. By implication, then, he claims the right to determine what activity is and is not appropriate on that day. He is the author of that law and therefore has the authority, with his Father, to make those determinations. What Jesus does not do in this exchange is to argue, explicitly or implicitly, that the Sabbath so finds its fulfillment in him that it is set to expire imminently. On the contrary, Jesus speaks of the Sabbath as a creation ordinance that continues to bind human beings.

Second, in John 7:22–24, Jesus once again defends his action of healing the paralytic on the Sabbath. Here he observes that his opponents "circumcise a man on the Sabbath" (7:22). Jesus does not dispute the lawfulness of this action (7:22). But, Jesus reasons, these opponents have no basis on which to be "angry with me because on the Sabbath I made a man's whole body well" (7:23). The sign of circumcision, then, points to the greater reality of spiritual healing and restoration, which Jesus's raising of the paralytic dramatizes. If one may perform the sign on the Sabbath, then one may certainly perform the reality on the Sabbath. Thus, in pointing out this inconsistency between his opponents' actions on the Sabbath and their criticisms of his own actions on the Sabbath, Jesus once again defends his healing as an activity that is appropriate to the Sabbath day.

Third, in John 9:1–41, Jesus heals a man born blind. He does so in a striking way—he "spit on the ground and made mud with the saliva. Then he anointed the man's eyes with the mud and said to him,

---

17. Moisés Silva, ed., "sabbaton," in *New International Dictionary of New Testament Theology and Exegesis*, ed. Moises Silva (Grand Rapids, MI: Zondervan, 2014), 225.

'Go, wash in the pool of Siloam' (which means Sent). So he went and washed and came back seeing" (9:6–7). The Pharisees take note that Jesus "made the mud and opened [the man's] eyes" on the "Sabbath day" (9:14), and then they declare, "This man is not from God, for he does not keep the Sabbath" (9:16). They judge his activities on the Sabbath to be in violation of it. The man, however, confesses Jesus, first as "a prophet" (9:17), then as "from God" (9:33), and finally as "the Son of Man" (9:35), at which point "he said, 'Lord, I believe,' and he worshiped him" (9:38). Thus, the blind man has received not only his physical sight but also spiritual sight; he comes to understand who Jesus truly is and worships him in light of that revelation. The Pharisees, on the other hand, although fully capable of seeing with their physical eyes, are blind spiritually (9:40–41).

In light of that conclusion, John shows us that the Pharisees' criticism of Jesus is misdirected. Their accusation that Jesus is a Sabbath breaker proceeds from spiritual blindness. Jesus's opponents do not understand him nor, by implication, do they understand the law of God. The fact that the healed man comes to worship Jesus in light of his self-revelation (cf. 9:38) simply confirms the fact that his healing of that man was a fitting thing to do on the Sabbath. In fact, the healed man's worship of Jesus is precisely the aim and purpose of the Sabbath—that human beings would engage in the holy resting of worshipping their Creator and Redeemer.

Overall, what John shows us in these three brief treatments of the Sabbath is that, in Jerusalem no less than in Galilee, Jesus was criticized for allegedly breaking the Sabbath. In each and every case, Jesus defends his actions as appropriate to the Sabbath. Furthermore, he reminds us of the origins and purpose of the Sabbath at the creation. In John 5, Jesus argues for his own equality with the God who instituted the Sabbath at the creation, and in John 9, he receives the worship of a man he had healed on the Sabbath. What particularly scandalizes Jesus's contemporaries throughout John's Gospel is that Jesus claims to be the God who created the world and who made human beings to worship and have fellowship with him. Yet, it is precisely because these claims are true that John authored his Gospel and bids us to join in the worship of Jesus Christ, the Son of God (see 20:30–31).

Conclusions

Jesus's earthly ministry affords rich materials for addressing God's purposes for the Sabbath in creation and redemption. We have seen that he ministers squarely in an Old Testament context as the Mosaic covenant remained in force for the duration of his life and ministry (until his resurrection from the dead). Thus, Jesus's stance toward the Sabbath is precisely what we expect it would be—entirely positive. In our survey of his statements about and activity on the Sabbath, we have observed three lines of teaching emerging from the four Gospels.

First, Jesus both affirms the Sabbath as a divine commandment and clarifies its true meaning. He explicitly affirms that it is a command that God gave at the creation (Mark 2:27; John 5:17), and the many accounts of Jesus's presence in synagogues on the Sabbath demonstrate his commitment to honor the command by joining with God's people in corporate worship. He thereby reaffirms the primary purpose of the Sabbath, which is to draw human beings into the presence of God to worship him. Jesus emphasizes that the Sabbath is for man's benefit (Mark 2:27) and is a day appointed for doing good (Matt. 12:12). The day, then, is a blessing—not a curse—for humanity.

In defending himself and his disciples against the criticisms of various Jewish leaders, Jesus frees the Sabbath from human traditions and other extralegal additions. Only the divine legislator, not mere human beings, has the right to say what is and is not proper activity on this day. Thus, in addition to gathered worship, which is the primary occupation of the day, Jesus points to two more kinds of activity that are permissible on the Sabbath. First, when his disciples are accompanying him in the work of ministry and find themselves hungry on their travels on the Sabbath, Jesus defends their right to feed themselves (Mark 2:23–28). They should attend to this physical necessity of relieving hunger with an entirely clear conscience. Second, Jesus offers illustration after illustration of performing works of mercy on the Sabbath toward those in need (Mark 1:21–28, 29–31; 3:1–6; Luke 13:10–17, 14:1–6; John 5:1–18; 9:1–41). As opportunities to show mercy on the Sabbath arise in the providence of God, Jesus stresses, one ought not to hesitate nor to delay to do such works.

Second, during his earthly ministry Jesus affirms his lordship over the Sabbath (Mark 2:28; John 5:17). He is lord over the Sabbath as the Messianic Son of Man, and he is lord over the Sabbath as the divine lawgiver. Jesus does not abolish or abrogate the Sabbath. On the contrary, he affirms his authority over it and asserts his right to declare how human beings should honor this day.

Third, Jesus's teaching and ministry in relation to the Sabbath highlight an important emphasis in the Old Testament's testimony to the Sabbath—the Sabbath was a day to remember God's deliverance of his people from bondage in Egypt. Tellingly, in his inaugural sermon, given on the Sabbath, Jesus not only proclaims "liberty to the captives" but also says that he has been "sent . . . to set at liberty those who are oppressed" (Luke 4:18). A new exodus will come about through the life, death, and resurrection of Christ. Thus, Jesus's Sabbath miracles deliver men and women who are possessed by the devil (Mark 1:21–28; Luke 13:10–17) and who are afflicted by various illnesses and maladies (Mark 1:29–31; Mark 3:1–6; Luke 14:1–6; John 5:1–18; 9:1–41). They point to Jesus's mission of living, dying, and rising again in order to save sinners from sin and to bring them to eternal life. This trajectory is particularly evident in the healing of the man born blind. Jesus restores his physical sight on the Sabbath, but Jesus also gives him spiritual sight—by faith he worships Christ. In this way, Jesus shows us how his mission is intended to realize God's purposes for the Sabbath at the creation of the world—he will redeem a multitude of human beings who will worship their Maker and their Redeemer.

As we saw above, Jesus's dialogue with the Samaritan woman hints at a significant transformation of worship that will come with the arrival of his "hour" (John 4:21–24). Once he is raised from the dead, the age of fulfillment formally breaks into history. Thus, in the next chapter, we will explore what implications the resurrection of Jesus Christ has for the Sabbath.

5

New Creation

According to the New Testament, the resurrection of Jesus Christ from the dead is a dividing line in human history. As such, it cannot but have implications for the Sabbath. In this chapter we are going to explore the testimony of the New Testament to the Sabbath in the period of history between the resurrection of Christ and the return of Christ at the end of the age. We will first explore the resurrection accounts in the Gospels, which give us an important and immediate clue to the implications of the resurrection for the Sabbath. We will then look at what Acts, the Letters, and Revelation tell us about the Sabbath in the early church. Finally, we will explore the place of the Sabbath in the New Testament's teaching about the law in the Christian life.

The Gospels and the Sabbath
"The First Day of the Week"

The Gospels are united in reporting that Jesus rose from the dead on the first day of the week. Luke's account is particularly instructive. He tells us that when "the women who had come with [Jesus] from

Galilee" arrive at the tomb "on the first day of the week," they find the tomb empty (Luke 23:55; 24:1). "Two men . . . in dazzling apparel" meet them and inform them that Jesus "has risen" (24:4, 6), reminding the women of what Jesus had said in his earthly ministry, that he would "be crucified and on the third day rise" (24:7; cf. 24:1, 13, 21). Thus, it is not simply that the women learn of the resurrection of Jesus on the first day of the week—Jesus has himself been raised from the dead on the first day of the week.

In addition to this, Jesus appears to his disciples on the first day of the week several times. Three of these appearances come in immediate succession toward the end of John's Gospel and the other two appearances are recorded in Luke. John tells us that Mary Magdalene, "on the first day of the week, . . . came to the tomb early" (John 20:1). She discovers that the tomb is empty and tells Peter and John, "They have taken the Lord out of the tomb, and we do not know where they have laid him" (20:2). This (false) assumption prompts her to weep outside the empty tomb (20:11). After "two angels" sitting in the tomb ask Mary why she is weeping, Jesus appears to her, though she does not recognize him (20:12–15). It is only when Jesus addresses Mary by name that she sees it is him (20:16; cf. 10:16, 27). Jesus then tells her, "Do not cling to me, for I have not yet ascended to the Father" (20:17).

Thus, this passage shows that the resurrection marks a new mode of communion between Jesus and his disciples. Up to this point, Jesus's disciples have had fellowship with him through the five senses. From now on, until he returns in glory, disciples will commune with Jesus exclusively by the ministry of the Holy Spirit—whom Jesus will receive from the Father and send in power to his people (see 14:16; 15:26)—and through the word of Christ (14:23). But this is not a lesser kind of fellowship; in fact, Jesus had earlier said that it is far better than what they had previously enjoyed with him (16:7).

Overall, this first resurrection appearance in John's account is important for a number of reasons. It shows us that Christ was raised from the dead on the first day of the week. It shows us that he also appeared to Mary Magdelene on that day, appointing her as a witness to the disciples that Christ had been raised from the dead (20:17–18). And it gives us a glimpse into the kind of fellowship that Christ will enjoy with his disciples between his resurrection and return.

It is this fellowship that John emphasizes in his description of a second resurrection appearance of Christ. On this occasion, Christ appears to ten of his disciples (20:19–23). John makes a point of telling us that Jesus met with these disciples "on the evening of that day, the first day of the week" (20:19). He declares to them, "Peace be with you," then "showed them his hands and his side," and again declared his "peace" to them (20:19, 20, 21). This "peace" is a fruit of Christ's finished work of redemption. By his death and resurrection, he reconciles sinners to God. Formerly enemies of God, now, in Christ, they are friends of God. This "peace" is a blessing that they enjoy through faith in Christ. It will be this message of peace that the disciples must soon take to the nations (see 20:21–23). In showing the disciples "his hands and his side," Jesus furnishes them with evidence of his resurrection—in the very same body in which he died, he has been raised gloriously to life (20:20)—because he wants them with to have every confidence that the peace they have in Christ and that they offer to the nations is a well-grounded one. Its foundation lies in the death and resurrection of Jesus Christ.

In summary, when the disciples were gathered together on "the evening of that day, the first day of the week" (20:19), Jesus blesses that gathering with his presence and with the pronouncement of the peace that he has secured by his death and resurrection and that they enjoy through faith in him. Furthermore, he commissions them to proclaim Christ as Savior to the nations in the power of the Spirit. Thus, the presence of Christ with his people and the proclamation of the gospel to gather sinners and to edify the people of God are marks or traits of this "first day of the week."

That these marks or traits are not unique to this particular "first day of the week" finds confirmation in what John next tells us (20:24–29). He first parenthetically mentions Thomas's absence from that earlier gathering and his skepticism about the other disciples' reports of Jesus's resurrection (20:24–25). He then relates a subsequent gathering—John 20:26 reads, "Eight days later, his disciples were inside again, and Thomas was with them."[1] Thus, it is the first day of the week, one week after Jesus's initial appearance to his disciples. Jesus again meets with the disciples and declares, "Peace be with you" (20:26), and he invites Thomas to witness for himself that he has been raised from the dead. Thomas then confesses, "My Lord and my God!" (20:28). In response, Jesus pronounces his blessing upon "those who have not seen and yet have believed" (20:29), and John concludes that the reason he penned this Gospel is so that readers "may believe that Jesus is the Christ, the Son of God, and that by believing [they] may have life in his name" (20:31). Once again, the presence of Christ with his people and the proclamation of the gospel to gather sinners and to edify the people of God characterize the "first day of the week."

Two further accounts of a resurrection appearance of Christ to his disciples on the first day of the week are found in Luke 24:13–35 and Luke 24:36–43. First, Luke tells us that on "that very day" (Luke 24:13)—the day Christ was raised from the dead (Luke 24:1–12)—two disciples were traveling from Jerusalem to Emmaus. Jesus "drew

---

1. "Eight days" is one week by inclusive reckoning. It is therefore exactly one week later.

near and went with them[, b]ut their eyes were kept from recognizing him" (24:13, 15–16). After these two disciples relate what has "happened [in Jerusalem] in these days" (24:18), Jesus rebukes them, saying, "Was it not necessary that the Christ should suffer these things and enter into his glory?" (24:26). He then, "beginning with Moses and all the Prophets, . . . interpreted to them in all the Scriptures the things concerning himself" (24:27).

Jesus travels on farther with these two disciples, and they sit down to a meal. Then "when he was at table with them, he took the bread and blessed and broke it and gave it to them" (24:30). It is at that point that "their eyes were opened, and they recognized him. And he vanished from their sight" (24:31). They immediately "returned to Jerusalem" and announced to "the eleven" disciples that "the Lord has risen indeed" and that "he was known to them in the breaking of the bread" (24:33, 34, 35).

This "first day of the week" appearance shares many of the same features in common with the accounts in John: Jesus meets with his disciples, he tells them of his finished, saving work and its implications for their lives, and the disciples declare to others that Jesus has been raised. There is one detail in this account, however, that is unique among the Sunday resurrection appearances—on this occasion, Jesus revealed himself to the Emmaus disciples "in the breaking of the bread" (24:35). The last occasion when Jesus broke bread with disciples was the Last Supper, when he instituted the Lord's Supper as an ordinance of the new covenant (22:14–23). Thus, at this meal in Emmaus, we get a glimpse of what the bread and the cup in the Lord's Supper signify and seal—fellowship in the body and blood of Christ (cf. 1 Cor. 10:16). Although it is doubtful that this particular meal is an observance of the Supper, it nevertheless stands alongside the Supper as an occasion when the risen Christ was pleased to commune with his disciples.

Luke's second account of Christ's resurrection appearances to his disciples occurs immediately after this meal (Luke 24:36–43).[2] This account is likely parallel to the resurrection appearance of Christ to the ten disciples in John 20:19–23. When Jesus appears, he "sa[ys] to them, 'Peace to you!'" (Luke 24:36). Because the disciples think that they have seen "a spirit," Jesus reassures them that it is him, raised from the dead in the same body in which he suffered and died (24:37), by showing them "his hands and his feet" and eating "a piece of broiled fish" in their presence (24:40, 42–43). As in other accounts, including John 20:19–23, Jesus announces redemptive blessing to his disciples and then proceeds to show its historical grounding—his finished saving work accomplished in his death on the cross and his resurrection from the dead.

From these five "first day of the week" postresurrection accounts, a harmonious, composite picture emerges. First, and very simply, the risen Jesus appeared to his disciples several times on the first day of the week. Luke and John take care to document four distinct appearances of Christ to his disciples on the first day of the week. This is not to suggest that Christ did not appear to his disciples on any other day. Other appearances, after all, are undated (Luke 24:44–49, 50–53; John 21:1–25; Matt. 28:16–20). But the only dated resurrection appearances in the New Testament fall on the first day of the week. Luke and John do not, then, regard this particular day to be incidental to the meaning and significance of what they relate to us.

Second, there are details that are common to these "first day of the week" appearances. Four of the five begin with multiple disciples gathered together. In most of them, Jesus furnishes proof or evidence that he has been raised bodily from the dead. In all of them, Jesus

---

2. Luke tells us that these two disciples "rose that same hour" after Jesus had "vanished from their sight" (24:33, 31). They immediately "returned to Jerusalem" and reported to the "eleven and those who were with them gathered together" what they had seen and heard (24:33, 34–35). It was at that point that Jesus appeared (24:36).

communes with his disciples by his word. He proclaims to them the saving benefits of his redemptive work ("peace"). He sets his redemptive ministry of suffering and glory in the context of the testimony of Moses and the Prophets. He commissions his disciples to proclaim the good news about his death and resurrection to others, offering forgiveness in his name. And, in the case of the two Emmaus disciples, he reveals himself in context of the breaking of bread.

When these details are read against the backdrop of the whole of the New Testament, an unmistakable pattern emerges—they all reflect the public worship of God within the apostolic church. As we will see below, disciples gathered on the first day of the week, under the supervision of the apostles, to worship God. Preeminent in this gathered worship was the preaching of the word. On this day, believers also observed the Lord's Supper. What characterized these assemblies most of all was the presence of God with his people (1 Cor. 14:25).

Overall, these details closely match what transpired when Christ appeared to his disciples on the first day of the week. Thus, they suggest a transformation in the way that people are to worship God under the new covenant. Disciples continue to gather one day a week in order to worship God. This weekly public worship is an abiding feature of the life of God's new covenant people. What has changed, according to the New Testament writers, is the particular day on which believers assemble to worship God. From the creation until the resurrection, God called people to worship him on the seventh day of the week. From the resurrection until the return of Christ, God calls people to worship him on the first day of the week.

FROM SEVENTH TO FIRST

This raises the question, "why?" Why is it that, at the resurrection, God shifts the day when people are to rest from the labors of their earthly callings and to gather in his worship? To answer this question, we first need to think about the significance of the resurrection according to the New Testament. The resurrection has momentous implications for human history. Paul tells us that the saving work of Christ brings history to its intended climax and consummation (Gal. 4:4; Eph. 1:10). For this reason, he links Jesus's resurrection with the eschatological age to come (Eph. 1:20–23). On the day of Pentecost, the risen Christ poured out the Holy Spirit in fullness upon the crowds gathered in Jerusalem, and Peter told them that this outpouring of the Spirit by the risen Christ meant that "the last days" had dawned (Acts 2:17). The New Testament further shows us the epochal significance of the resurrection of Christ by relating the resurrection to creation. Paul tells the Colossians that Christ is both "the firstborn of all creation" and "the firstborn from the dead" (Col. 1:15, 18). This parallel expression shows Paul's understanding of "the resurrection as a new cosmic beginning."[3] Similarly, when writing to the Corinthians, Paul links Jesus's resurrection with the "new creation" (2 Cor. 5:15–17).[4] Thus, the resurrection of Christ from the dead is a watershed moment in human history. It is the dawn of the last days and of the age to come—the consummation of human history. It stands parallel to the creation of the world in its significance and scope.

Overall, understanding what the resurrection is and means for human history helps us to understand its implications for the Sabbath. The Sabbath, we have seen, is a creation ordinance. God instituted it at the creation so that human beings might remember God's creation of the world in six days. By setting the Sabbath on the seventh day, God was showing humanity his goal for human

---

3. G. K. Beale, *New Testament Biblical Theology: The Unfolding of the Old Testament in the New* (Grand Rapids, MI: Baker, 2011), 339.

4. Beale, *New Testament Biblical Theology*, 339.

existence—the worship of him who made all things. Later, in Deuteronomy, the Sabbath comes to take on added significance as God tells Israel that it is a day to remember how he redeemed them from bondage in Egypt.

Connected to both of these purposes, the resurrection is equally the dawn of the new creation in human history and part of the unique, once-for-all work of Christ to save sinners from among the nations. In fact, all those and only those whom Christ has redeemed by his life, death, and resurrection are given entrance into the new creation (2 Cor. 5:17). In this way, God is bringing his purposes for humanity to realization. It is by the work of the last Adam, the second man, that God redeems sinners in every age. And this new humanity, forged in Christ, communes with the triune God through faith in Christ.

The Sabbath, then, comes to commemorate God's work of new creation and redemption in the resurrection of Christ. There continues to be one day in seven when God's people lay down their earthly labors and commitments and gather together to worship God. Thus the substance of the command is unchanged. However, the particular day does change. Beginning at the resurrection, the appointed day for God's people to assemble in the holy resting of worship is Sunday. On this first day of the week, we are to remember that Christ was raised from the dead. In Christ, we have witnessed God's purposes for the creation come to fulfillment and fruition and we engage in that for which we were made—worship of our great God.[5] We also remember that, by his death and resurrection, Christ redeemed a multitude of sinners. What the exodus anticipated in shadow form, Christ has accomplished in his saving work. Thus, on the first day of the week, we look back in grateful remembrance on the fact that Christ was

---

5. Of course, the people of God worshipped him before Christ's resurrection as well.

"raised for our justification" (Rom. 4:25) and that, in union with the risen Christ, we have been brought from death to life (Eph. 2:5–6).

But if, on the first day of the week, we look back upon Christ's resurrection as the inbreaking of new creation into human history and as the saving victory of God to redeem his people, we no less look forward. The Sabbath, in other words, continues to be eschatological in nature. The new creation has been inaugurated in Christ but not yet consummated. Redemption has been fully accomplished, once for all, but it will not be fully applied to all the elect until Christ returns in glory. United with Christ, believers have already begun to share in his resurrection. But we have yet to experience all that he has won for us in his resurrection. The resurrection of the body, in conformity with Christ's resurrection body, is the sure and certain hope of every Christian (1 Cor. 15:35–58; 1 Thess. 4:13–18; Phil. 3:21). And the "redemption of our bodies," Paul tells us, is of a piece with the renewal of the whole creation (Rom. 8:23; see Rom. 8:18–25). Fully redeemed, we will dwell with God in Christ in new heavens and new earth.

In light of what the resurrection means—for Christ, for believers, and for God's purposes in human history—we are better able to appreciate why God moved the Sabbath from the seventh day of the week to the first day of the week when Christ rose from the dead. God's work of creation and redemption finds its center and culmination in the person and work of Jesus Christ. The consummation of God's purposes for humanity and the world has found its beginnings in the death and resurrection of Christ. It is on Sunday, then, when people are to look back to what God has done in Christ and to look forward to what God will certainly do in Christ. Fittingly, on the very first Sabbath under the new covenant—the day on which Christ was raised from the dead—we see Christ meeting in fellowship with his people, we see the word of Christ bringing blessing, instruction, guidance, and direction to his people, and we see the people of God assembled to worship the Savior. It is precisely these features that will characterize the life of the early church on the first day of the week. Thus, we may now turn to explore what Acts, the Letters, and Revelation tell us about the Sabbath under the new covenant.

Acts, the Letters, Revelation, and the Sabbath

ACTS

In Acts, we see the church developing from a handful of Jewish believers to a multinational body numbering in the tens of thousands. By the authoritative command of the risen Christ (Acts 1:8) and the power of the Spirit of Christ (1:5, 8), the apostles carry the gospel from the Jew to the Samaritan to the rest of the nations (1:8). The apostle whom Christ preeminently tasks with extending the gospel to the Gentiles is Paul (9:15; 22:21; 26:17). Paul consistently made it a point to present the gospel to Jewish audiences when he first arrived in a new location; he would find the local synagogue and preach Christ there. Luke, in fact, tells us that this was Paul's "custom" (17:2). For this reason, Paul was often found on the Jewish Sabbath in the synagogues of the cities where he was preaching. Typically, his preaching met with both acceptance and resistance. And this resistance occasioned two important steps on the part of Paul. First, he would signal his commitment to take the gospel to the Gentiles. Second, he would gather those who had accepted Christ and form a distinct community of those who had professed faith in Christ and of their families. This is precisely the trajectory of Paul's ministry in Corinth (18:5–8) and it was likely replicated in other cities as well.

However, Luke is clear that in separating from the synagogue, the church in no way repudiates the Scriptures of the Old Testament. On the contrary, the Old Testament finds its intended fulfillment in the person and work of Christ (see Luke 24:25–27, 44–49). Thus, the apostles preach Christ to Jewish audiences from the Scriptures of the Old Testament (see, representatively, Acts 17:2–3), and when Jewish audiences reject Jesus Christ, they are rejecting their Scriptures and the God who authored those Scriptures. This is one reason why Christians in Acts form communities distinct from existing synagogues. Baptized into Christ, disciples live out their faith and life together in the church. Together they take up the mission that Christ has entrusted to his church—to carry the name of Jesus into the world and to live under the lordship of Christ.

One feature that is constant to the churches that Luke describes in Acts is that they are worshipping communities. We see them gathered in prayer (Acts 1:14; 4:23–31; 12:12) and under the ministry of the preached word (see 19:9; 20:20, 21, 27). Luke tells us that, from the beginning, the disciples "devoted themselves to the apostles' teaching and the fellowship, to the breaking of bread and the prayers" (2:42). Because Luke is primarily concerned to document the extension of the gospel from the Jews to the nations, we have comparatively few details about the services of gathered worship in the early churches. But we do have one such account, and we are likely intended to take it as representative of the church's public worship under the supervision of the apostles.

In Acts 20, toward the end of Paul's last documented missionary journey in Acts, Paul gathers with the church in Troas. Luke—who was accompanying Paul on that journey—says, "we were gathered together to break bread," a reference to the Lord's Supper (20:7; cf. 1 Cor. 10:16; 11:23, 24). Further, before they observed the Supper, Paul "prolonged his speech until midnight" (20:7)—that is to say, he preached the word of God before he administered the Supper to the church (20:11). Thus, overall, word and sacrament characterized the public worship of the churches of Jesus Christ.

There is one further detail about this particular gathering that helps us to understand the pattern of Christian worship at the dawn of the new covenant—Luke tells us that the church in Troas gathered "on the first day of the week" (20:7). This expression is also found in Luke 24:1 and in John 20:1 (cf. 20:19). Its use in Acts, therefore, points to this particular day as having special significance in the Christian church.

One might suppose that perhaps the church met on this day because it was convenient to the itinerary of the apostle Paul. After all, we learn later that Paul is "hastening to be at Jerusalem, if possible, on the day of Pentecost" (Acts 20:16). However, when we look more closely at Paul's itinerary, a different picture emerges. Paul is indeed in a hurry to be in Jerusalem by Pentecost. His trip from Philippi (in Macedonia) to Troas (in northwestern Asia Minor) took "five days" (20:6). Previously, Paul had sailed from Troas to Philippi in just two days (16:11). Adverse winds likely accounted for the delay. Yet, his haste and this deficit of time notwithstanding, Luke tells us that Paul and his fellow travelers "stayed [in Troas] for seven days" (20:6).

So why did Paul spend an additional seven days in Troas, given his tight schedule? The answer comes in the following verse. Paul was waiting to gather with the church in Troas "on the first day of the week" (20:7). The "first day of the week" was, of course, the day on which Christ had been raised from the dead. And, under the new covenant, it is now the particular day on which God's people observe the weekly holy resting that he had required of them since creation. Thus, Paul does not call the church to gather for public worship on an earlier day, even though that would have been far more convenient for him, but arranges his travel schedule so that he can observe that day in worship with the church.

Overall, these events confirm that in the early church, the first day of the week had been set by divine authority. And because there is nothing in this account that suggests that what transpired on this Sunday in Troas was peculiar either to the circumstances of the church or to the location of this particular church, it seems this practice was one universally embraced by the apostolic churches and intended for the church in every place and in every age. This conclusion finds confirmation from the Letters of the New Testament, to which we now turn.

LETTERS

There are two passages in the Epistles of the New Testament that, in different ways, point to the first day of the week as the day when local churches were to gather to worship God by divine command. The first comes from Paul's first letter to the Corinthians when he writes,

> Now concerning the collection for the saints: as I directed the churches of Galatia, so you also are to do. On the first day of every week, each of you is to put something aside and store it up, as he may prosper, so that there will be no collecting when I come. And when I arrive, I will send those whom you accredit by letter to carry your gift to Jerusalem. If it seems advisable that I should go also, they will accompany me. (1 Cor. 16:1–4)

Here, Paul is likely taking up a question or concern that has come to him from the church.[6] He mentions a "collection for the saints" (16:1), and the Corinthians seem to already be familiar with it. This collection is one that Paul is gathering from the Corinthians, the Galatians, and the churches in Macedonia (see 2 Cor. 8–9). As Paul

---

6. A point rightly captured by the ESV's explanatory note, "The expression *Now concerning* introduces a reply to a question in the Corinthians' letter." *ESV Study Bible*, ed. Wayne Grudem (Wheaton, IL: Crossway, 2008), 2216n1.

explains in his letter to the church in Rome, this collection will be an expression of fellowship and unity between its givers (predominantly Gentile churches) and its recipients (the predominantly Jewish churches in Judea) (see Rom. 15:22–33).

In these verses, Paul tells the Corinthians that he wants this collection to be taken up in the same way that he had told the "churches of Galatia" to take it up (1 Cor. 16:1). In particular, the collection is to be gathered from willing givers in the church "on the first day of every week" (16:2). This appears to be a regular provision for the church—until Paul arrives in Corinth, the Corinthians are to be taking up the collection on a weekly basis.

But why does Paul instruct churches in two different regions (Achaia and Galatia) to take up the collection "on the first day of the week"? The reason is because he knows that these churches—just like the others—are already gathering together on that day for worship. The day's significance, of course, derives from the fact that it is the day on which Christ rose from the dead.

Thus, it is likely that Paul intends the taking up of this collection to be a part of the public worship of God in the church on the first day of the week. As an act of worship, the members of the church generously give what they have thoughtfully prepared beforehand to give. In this instance, the collection will serve to meet the temporal needs of brothers in another part of the church. And even after the collection is gathered and disbursed, Paul likely expects the churches to continue to take up a collection in public worship to support, among other benevolences and ministries, the genuine needs of fellow Christians. As under the Old Testament, so under the New Testament—God wants his people to worship him from hearts that are sensitive to the earthly needs of others, particularly fellow believers, and are willing to take concrete and practical steps to address those needs. As we have already seen in Isaiah, the worship of God is primarily vertical, but it has an indispensable horizontal component to it; the love of God may never be divorced from the love of one's brothers and sisters in Christ.

A second passage that points to the regular, weekly gathering of the church for public worship is Hebrews 10:24–25, which exhorts believers to "consider how to stir up one another to love and good works, not neglecting to meet together, as is the habit of some, but encouraging one another, and all the more as you see the Day drawing near." The core of this exhortation is that they are not to "neglect" to "meet together." Since the author to the Hebrews delivers this command to his audience without qualification, we are safe in concluding that it pertains to the whole church—that is to say, the church is under a divine command to assemble.

This command derives a certain urgency from the fact that "some" are in the "habit" of neglecting to gather. The writer does not tell us exactly who these people are or specify the details or motives of such failure to gather with the church in these meetings; he only says that it is a standing or habitual neglect. The writer is clear, however, that this behavior is a violation of a divine command.

To be sure, the writer does not specify exactly when the church is to "meet together." But, in the context of the teaching of the New Testament as a whole, it is almost certain that he has in mind the gathering of the church for worship on the first day of the week. As we have seen above, this was the practice of the churches in Troas, Galatia, and Corinth, churches that were under the supervision of the apostle Paul. This practice, furthermore, was a matter of obedience to a command of the risen Lord Jesus Christ.

In addition to the exhortation to gather, the writer of Hebrews also describes what he expects will happen on this particular day when the church gathers, and these details confirm the conclusion that the meeting in view here is the regular gathering of the church for worship on Sunday. First, this is a day when believers "stir up one another to love and good works," when they "encourag[e] one another." Such activity takes place in the context of the fellowship of believers and is the fruit of the ministry of the preached word in the church. The word supplies both the commands ("love," "good works") and gospel motivation ("encourag[ement]") that enable believers to undertake this ministry to one another. Furthermore, the singing of "psalms and hymns and spiritual songs" is the "content (or possibly manner) of the 'teaching and admonishing'" in Colossians 3:16.[7] Thus, when God's word is sung in public worship, believers are instructing and encouraging one another. It is in these ways, then, that the writer is urging his audience to be faithful in attending and participating in the public worship of the church so that they may urge one another on to fruitful living for Christ.

Second, the writer tells the Hebrews to commit to regular, gathered worship because "the Day [is] drawing near" (10:25). This "day" is, of course, the return of Christ in glory. As the writer goes on to say, it will be characterized by judgment and condemnation to those who do not truly belong to Jesus Christ (Heb. 10:26–31), but it will also be a day when God's people fully enter into their "better" and "abiding" "possession" and "receive what is promised" (10:34, 36). It is this prospect, the writer reasons, that should motivate believers to engage in the regular, gathered worship of God on the first day of the week.

Strikingly, the writer has earlier termed this hope of the Christian a "Sabbath rest" that "remains . . . for the people of God" (4:9). It is this future "rest" into which every believer will enter when Christ returns in glory on that "day" (4:10; 10:25). As we saw earlier, calling

---

7. G. K. Beale, *Colossians and Philemon*, Baker Exegetical Commentary on the New Testament (Grand Rapids, MI: Baker, 2019), 303.

this rest a "Sabbath" rest indicates that the creation ordinance of the weekly Sabbath continues under the new covenant. It points to the eschatological life in Jesus Christ that believers have yet to experience in full. The weekly Sabbath, then, serves to point believers to their heavenly hope so that they may strive toward it along the path of faith and good works.

Thus, although the writer of Hebrews does not use either the term "rest" or "Sabbath" in his argument in chapter 10, his lines of argumentation in chapters 4 and 10 run on parallel tracks and serve to complement and reinforce one another. The return of Christ is the hoped for "day" when believers will receive their "possession," "reward," and "rest" (10:34, 35; 4:9). Presently, believers are on pilgrimage and therefore require "endurance" in the way of "faith" (10:36, 39); they need to "strive to enter that rest" through "faith" (4:11, 2). So, as a help to believers, God calls his people to gather together weekly (10:25; cf. 4:9). These weekly gatherings serve, by the grace of God, to "stir up" believers "to love and good works" and to "encourag[e]" them (10:24, 25)—that is to say, God intends those meetings to be precisely the help that pilgrims need as they make their way toward their heavenly home. The final book of the New Testament, Revelation, helps us understand the foundation and effects of such encouragement more fully.

Revelation

Revelation opens with the apostle John in exile on the island of Patmos (Rev. 1:9). He hears an authoritative voice (1:10–11) and sees a vision of the exalted Christ (1:12–16) while he "was in the Spirit on the Lord's day" (1:10). The expression "Lord's day" is otherwise unattested in the New Testament, although later Christians would soon pick up the phrase to designate Sunday as the weekly day of Christian worship, but we may reliably draw some conclusions about this phrase's meaning by attending to a few details in this verse and its surrounding context.[8]

First, the adjective "Lord's" (*kyriakos*) appears in one other place in the New Testament ("the *Lord's* supper," 1 Cor. 11:20). In both places, it likely denotes possession. In other words, the "supper" or "day" in view is one that belongs particularly to the Lord; he lays unique, proprietary claim to that meal and period of time. In the case of the phrase in Revelation 1:10, John is saying that Jesus Christ has set this day apart from the other six days of the week. The phrase "the Lord's day" thus "simply means the day belonging to the Lord."[9]

Second, the immediate context of the phrase helps to clarify and to sharpen our understanding of its meaning and significance. After hearing the authoritative voice, John sees a vision of Jesus Christ. He writes,

> Then I turned to see the voice that was speaking to me, and on turning I saw seven golden lampstands, and in the midst of the lampstands one like a son of man, clothed with a long robe and with a golden sash around his chest. The hairs of his head were white, like white wool, like snow. His eyes were like a flame of fire, his feet were like burnished bronze, refined in a furnace, and his voice was like the roar of many waters. In his right hand he held seven stars, from his mouth came a sharp two-edged sword, and his face was like the sun shining in full strength. (Rev. 1:12–16)

---

8. See the discussion of the second-century evidence in R. J. Bauckham, "The Lord's Day," in *From Sabbath to Lord's Day: A Biblical, Historical and Theological Investigation*, ed. D. A. Carson (Grand Rapids, MI: Zondervan, 1982), 222–32. Bauckham concludes that "the use of *kyriakē* in the *Didache*, Ignatius, and the *Gospel of Peter* seems to presuppose a well-established usage, and in that case it is rather probable that *kyriakē hēmera* already meant Sunday in the reign of Domitian." Bauckham, "The Lord's Day," 232.

9. Roger T. Beckwith and Wilfrid Stott, *This is the Day: The Biblical Doctrine of the Christian Sunday* (London: Marshall, Morgan & Scott, 1978), 36.

After seeing Jesus, John then hears his voice saying, "Fear not, I am the first and the last, and the living one. I died, and behold I am alive forevermore, and I have keys of Death and Hades" (1:17–18).

Overall, what John sees is a vision of Jesus Christ in power and glory. When Jesus speaks to John, he identifies himself as one who has been raised gloriously from the dead, will never die again, and has absolute authority over death as the one who conquered death in his resurrection. This self-identification of Jesus underscores the fact that the one John sees in Revelation 1:12–16 is the powerful and glorious *risen* Christ.

This vision is precisely what John and his readers need to see. John, after all, is in exile on Patmos "on account of the word of God and the testimony of Jesus" (1:9). He has been punished by the civil authorities for his faith in Jesus. Further, John is not unique in his suffering for Jesus Christ—he identifies himself to his readers as "your brother and partner in the tribulation and the kingdom and the patient endurance that are in Jesus" (1:9). Thus, what all these suffering Christians need is a vision of the reigning, glorious, risen Christ who is sovereign over his church and the world.

But how does this setting and message help us to understand the meaning of the phrase "the Lord's day" in Revelation 1:10? This context shows us that the "Lord" of this day is the risen Lord Jesus Christ. In light of this pairing of the resurrection of Jesus Christ and a day Christ particularly claims for himself, it is difficult to avoid the conclusion that "the Lord's day" is the first day of the week, the day when Christ rose from the dead, and the day when Christians— under apostolic supervision—gathered together to worship God, remembering the resurrection of Jesus Christ.

Overall, this passage helps us to understand at least two basic characteristics of this day and of Christian worship on it. The first is that on this day, the church remembers that Jesus Christ has been raised from the dead and has conquered death and Hades; he is sovereign over all things. As the church experiences persecution and tribulation in the world, believers need this weekly reminder of the victory that Christ has already won, of his absolute lordship over anyone and anything that would threaten to harm them. The church needs this perspective in order to persevere faithfully in the face of threats both external and internal to the church (see 2:1–3:22). Thus, on this "Lord's day," the risen Christ gives his servant John a message for the church—"fear not" (1:17). Every time the church gathers to worship on the Lord's Day, then, they are reminded that they have no reason to fear the people and authorities who stand opposed to Christ and to his church.

Second, "it is through the corporate worship of the church that Christ's lordship is actually realized in the life of the church."[10] In other words, the church's willing and faithful obedience to this command of the Lord Jesus Christ is itself an expression of his absolute lordship. Further, as the word of Christ is proclaimed in the churches on the Lord's Day, believers are equipped to "confess Christ as Lord" in every area of their lives.[11] Thus, the Lord's Day visibly demonstrates Christ's lordship when his people gather to worship him, and as believers live in accordance with the word of Christ in their families, schools, places of work, and communities, they further give expression to the lordship of Christ in front of a watching world.

The Law, the Sabbath, and the Christian

As we have seen, the resurrection of Jesus Christ from the dead was an epochal event in human history. It marks the inbreaking of the age to come, the beginning of the last days, and the dawn of the new creation. As such, it transforms the worship of the people of God. They

---

10. Bauckham, "Lord's Day," 245.
11. Bauckham, "Lord's Day," 245.

continue to observe the weekly Sabbath rest that God had appointed for all people at the creation; Hebrews confirms that the eschatological Sabbath rest remains future to them, implying the continuation of the weekly Sabbath in anticipation of that rest. But the particular day of that rest has changed. From the creation to the resurrection of Christ, the Sabbath fell on the seventh day of the week. This day commemorated the completion of God's work of creation in six days. From the resurrection of Christ until his return, the Sabbath now falls on the first day of the week. This day commemorates the new creation that has dawned because of Christ's resurrection from the dead.

There is no command in the New Testament that explicitly spells out this change of day. We learn of this change, rather, in implicit ways. The Gospels show us not only that Christ was raised from the dead on the first day of the week but also that he met with his disciples on the first day of the week. The events that transpire during those meetings anticipate what the New Testament tells us happens when believers gather together each week to worship God—the ministry of the word, the breaking of bread, and the presence of Christ in spiritual blessing to his people. As we have seen in the Letters and Revelation, the church, under the supervision of Christ's apostles, met regularly on the first day of the week, the "Lord's day" (Rev. 1:10). And on this day Christian congregations worshiped God through the reading and preaching of the word, the administration of the Lord's Supper, and the taking up of a collection. Every indication from the New Testament is that churches observed this day in obedience to Jesus Christ.

The absence of an explicit Sabbath command in the New Testament letters (such as, "you shall keep the first day of the week as the Sabbath under the new covenant") has troubled some Christians enough for them to conclude that the New Testament's apparent silence points to an abrogation of the Sabbath under the new covenant.

However, we have argued in this chapter that the New Testament is not silent on the matter and offers multiple positive indications of the church's regular and widespread observance of the Sabbath as a divine command.

Further, there is an additional line of teaching in the New Testament that helps to confirm this conclusion—as the New Testament reflects on the implications of the finished work of Christ, it does so in relation to the Mosaic law. Thus, we will now briefly explore three passages that point us to the Decalogue (which, of course, includes the Sabbath command) to spell out Christian obligation under the new covenant. We will also address a few passages that some have taken to say that the Mosaic law (generally) or the Sabbath (particularly) has been abrogated under the new covenant.

The Decalogue

In at least two passages, the apostle Paul shows us that the Ten Commandments summarize the duty of the Christian under the new covenant. First, in Romans 13, Paul helps us to understand the relationship between love and the law of God when he writes,

> Owe no one anything, except to love each other, for the one who loves another has fulfilled the law. For the commandments, "You shall not commit adultery, You shall not murder, You shall not steal, You shall not covet," and any other commandment, are summed up in this word: "You shall love your neighbor as yourself." Love does no wrong to a neighbor; therefore love is the fulfilling of the law. (Rom. 13:8–10)

In this passage, Paul shows us that, far from there being any tension between love and the law of God, love actually fulfils the law. It is precisely through the keeping of God's commandments that believers love their neighbor (and love God). Further, Paul does not leave us in doubt as to what those commandments are. He quotes several of the Ten Commandments, and he quotes them in the form that they appear in the Decalogue ("You shall not commit adultery, You shall not murder, You shall not steal, You shall not covet"; see Ex. 20:13–17; Deut. 5:17–21). Paul understands this list to be representative and not exhaustive (as he adds "and any other commandment"). Thus, he sends us to the Ten Commandments to find the standards of Christian duty.

Paul does not cite any commandment from the Decalogue regarding our duty to God, including the Sabbath commandment. But the context of these verses affords a ready explanation for why Paul only mentions the portion of the Decalogue that addresses our duty to our fellow human beings—this section of Romans (Rom. 12:1–15:13) is overwhelmingly concerned with the Christian's duty toward other people, whether fellow believers, those outside the church, or the civil magistrate. Thus, Paul's omission of those laws in the Decalogue addressing our relationship with God should not be taken to mean that they are no longer binding on the Christian. In fact, given the ongoing normativity of the portion of the Decalogue summarized by the command to "love your neighbor as yourself," one may reasonably presume that the portion of the Decalogue summarized by the command to "love the Lord your God with all your heart and with all your soul and with all your mind" is no less binding (see Matt. 22:34–39).

The way in which Paul directs Christians to the Ten Commandments in Romans 13, then, speaks volumes about his understanding of the Sabbath commandment in the Christian life. Paul points the believer to the Ten Commandments as the rule or standard of Christian obedience. The Sabbath is among those Ten Commandments. Therefore, the Sabbath remains a commandment that God's people under the new covenant must observe.

A second passage offers a critical qualification to what we have observed from Paul's handling of the Ten Commandments in Romans 13:8–10. In Ephesians 6:1–3, Paul gives the children of the church in Ephesus specific direction, telling them, "obey your parents in the Lord, for this is right. 'Honor your father and mother' (this is the first commandment with a promise), 'that it may go well with you and that you may live long in the land.'"

As he did in Romans 13, Paul quotes the commandment to honor one's parents in the same form as the Decalogue (see Ex. 20:12; Deut. 5:16). That Paul is doing so intentionally is confirmed by the fact that he parenthetically comments, "this is the first commandment with a promise." He then goes on to supply the reason annexed to the commandment from Deuteronomy 5:16, "that it may go well with you and that you may live long in the land."

What is striking about Paul's citation of this promise is that while its original recipients were Israelites who had been redeemed from Egypt, the apostle applies it to the children of a largely Gentile congregation in western Asia Minor (see Eph. 2:11). In other words, the Ephesian children are neither Jewish (for the most part) nor inhabitants of Canaan. Tellingly, Paul does not cite the remainder of Deuteronomy 5:16, "the land that the LORD your God is giving you." Paul, then, understands the commandment and its promise to have a wider and more extensive application than it does for old covenant Israel. It is "valid not merely for the Jew who worships the Father in Jerusalem, but for all those true worshippers everywhere who worship him in spirit and in truth."[12]

In fact, the way Paul interprets and applies this particular commandment from the Decalogue is a window into how he interprets

---

12. B. B. Warfield, "The Sabbath in the Word of God," in *Selected Shorter Writings*, ed. John E. Meeter, 2 vols. (Phillipsburg, NJ: P&R, 1971, 1973), 1:323. Warfield renders the word translated "land" (ESV) as "earth." While this is a defensible translation of the underlying Greek word, one need not concur with Warfield's translation in order to affirm his argument here.

and applies each one of the Ten Commandments. Overall, his application reflects the momentous changes in redemptive history between Sinai and Calvary. The death and resurrection of Christ has meant that the law has come to fulfillment and has undergone transformation. And as a result, anything specific to the Israelites under old covenant (such as promises relating to the land of Canaan) has been correspondingly affected—that is to say, the law undergoes the changes necessary to reflect the fact that God's people, in the age of fulfillment, is comprised now both of Jews and Gentiles.

This transformation guides us in understanding how Paul approaches the Sabbath commandment—this commandment binds believers under the new covenant insofar as this commandment reflects transformation in light of the finished work of Christ. For the New Testament writers, including Paul (see 1 Cor. 16:2), that transformation entails a change of day. By divine appointment, the holy day of resting now falls on the first day of the week rather than the seventh day of the week. The commandment has not undergone any substantial changes, just as the commandment to honor one's father and mother has not undergone any substantial changes. The change, rather, is a circumstantial one, and it reflects the triumph and victory of Christ's resurrection, the dawn of the new creation in human history.

The apostle James confirms what we have seen in the apostle Paul—that believers are bound to the Ten Commandments as the standard of Christian duty under the new covenant. Similarly to Paul in Romans 13:8–10, James tells us, "if you really fulfill the royal law according to the Scripture, 'You shall love your neighbor as yourself,' you are doing well" (James 2:8). Love, in other words, is the fulfillment of the law of God. James then explains what he understands this law to be—he mentions two commands, "Do not commit adultery" and "Do not murder" (2:11), both of which are drawn from the

Decalogue. Thus, we can conclude that James understands the "royal law" (2:8)—that is, the "law of liberty" (2:12) to which Christians are held to account—to be the Decalogue.[13] Although James only mentions the commands governing adultery and murder, he "might have taken any others of the precepts of the Decalogue to illustrate his point—the Fourth as well as the Sixth or Seventh."[14]

An Objection

On the other hand, the apostle Paul makes statements in his letters that have suggested to some readers that he understands the Sabbath commandment to be abrogated under the new covenant. Here are some examples:

> Therefore let no one pass judgment on you in questions of food and drink, or with regard to a festival or a new moon or a Sabbath. These are a shadow of the things to come, but the substance belongs to Christ. (Col. 2:16–17)

> But now that you have come to know God, or rather to be known by God, how can you turn back again to the weak and worthless elementary principles of the world, whose slaves you want to be once more? You observe days and months and seasons and years! I am afraid I may have labored over you in vain. (Gal. 4:9–11)

> One person esteems one day as better than another, while another esteems all days alike. Each one should be fully convinced in his own mind. The one who observes the day, observes it in honor of the Lord. (Rom. 14:5–6)

---

13. "The Decalogue evidently lies in [James's] mind as a convenient summary of fundamental duty; and he says in effect that it is binding on us all, in all its precepts alike, because they all alike are from God and publish his holy will." Warfield, "The Sabbath," 315.

14. Warfield, "The Sabbath," 315.

Overall, each of the letters in which these statements appear reflects the confusion of some individuals concerning the Mosaic law. We may look at each of them in turn. First, in Colossae, there are teachers who are "pass[ing] judgment" on the Colossians "with regard to a festival or a new moon or a Sabbath." Paul declares these to be a "shadow" of the "substance," namely, Christ. As such, the church is not bound to observe these particular days. The phrase "a festival or a new moon or a Sabbath" is one that surfaces a number of times in the Old Testament (see 1 Chron. 23:31; 2 Chron. 2:4; 31:3; Neh. 10:33; Ezek. 45:17). It serves to describe the liturgical calendar that God gave to Israel in the Mosaic law. Importantly, "a Sabbath" is plural in the Greek (*sabbatōn*). It refers, then, strictly to the multiple feast days in Israel's calendar that God added to the weekly Sabbath. Thus, what Paul is telling the church in these verses is that the liturgical calendar in the Pentateuch has served its purpose now that Christ has come; believers are no longer under any obligation to observe it. Paul's comments, however, say nothing about the weekly Sabbath.

Similarly, the churches in Galatia were under the influence of teachers who were pressing the observance of the Mosaic law for their justification. Paul pens this letter to dissuade them from that teaching and to remind them of the gospel that he had preached to them and that they had believed. Here, Paul rebukes the church for "observ[ing] days and months and seasons and years" (Gal. 4:10). And again, in context, this expression refers to the liturgical calendar of the Mosaic law, which set apart periods of time for Israel's worship. Now that Christ has come (4:4), Paul reasons, Israel's calendar has fulfilled its purpose in redemptive history. Thus, for new covenant Christians to try to observe this calendar is a return to bondage.[15]

---

15. Paul sees the bondage in view in Galatians in two lights. There is the comparative bondage of God's people's existence under the Mosaic covenant relevant to their existence under the new covenant (Gal. 4:1–6). And there is the added bondage of attempting to keep the law for

Last, in the church in Rome, there was a division among believers whom Paul identifies as "weak in faith" and "strong" (Rom. 14:1; 15:1). This division centered around food (14:2) and the observance of days (14:5). Here, Paul views the individual who abstains from eating certain foods and who "observes one day as better than another" to be a believer, but one who is weak in faith (14:5). The coupling of dietary restrictions with calendrical observances suggests that the issue in the church in Rome concerns the keeping of the dietary laws and the liturgical calendar of the Mosaic law. Thus, for a third time, when Paul implicitly tells the Roman Christians that they are not divinely obligated to regard "one day as better than another," he is not talking about the weekly Sabbath—he is talking about the feasts and festivals of the Mosaic calendar. As in his letters to the churches in Galatia and Colossae, Paul helps the Roman Christians to understand that those aspects of the Mosaic legislation unique to Israel—such as laws regarding food, feasts, and festivals—are no longer binding under the new covenant.

Conclusions

Overall, the New Testament shows us that the resurrection of Christ effected a profound transformation of the Sabbath. The Sabbath, now observed on the first day of the week, commemorates the in-breaking of the new creation at Christ's resurrection. It continues to point to creation, redemption, and consummation, now in light of the finished work of Christ. The Sabbath commemorates God's work of creation, even as it points forward to the rest that awaits the people of God, and the Sabbath commemorates God's work of redemption shadowed in the exodus and accomplished in the death and resurrection of Christ. It is Christ, the second Adam, who brings

---

justification, something God never intended for Israel to do with the law that he gave them (see Gal. 5:1–6).

creation to its intended goal, and it is Christ who guarantees that each of his redeemed ones will enter into their appointed rest. In our final chapter, we will think about some implications that this biblical theology of the Sabbath has for the way that we read the Bible and live the Christian life.

6

Practice

The Sabbath spans the Bible, from Genesis to Revelation. It does not sit on the periphery of the Scriptures but touches the center of the biblical message—the purpose for which God created human beings; the resurrection of the Lord Jesus Christ; the heavenly hope of God's people. As such, the Sabbath provides a unique window into Scripture's teaching and the Christian life. In this concluding chapter, we will review what we have seen the Bible to say about the Sabbath. We will then think about some of the implications of that teaching for the life and worship of the church today.

The Sabbath: From Genesis to Revelation

We first meet the Sabbath in the opening chapters of the Bible. After God makes the world and everything in it within six days, he rests on the seventh day. In particular, "God blessed the seventh day and made it holy" (Gen. 2:3). He sets apart this day as one when, each week, human beings will lay down their earthly labors and take up a different kind of work—the worship of God. The Sabbath is a reminder that God's image bearers were created for fellowship with their Maker.

Later in Genesis 2, we see a covenant that God makes with Adam. The purpose of this covenant was that Adam would enter into permanent and heightened communion with God, that is to say, Sabbath rest. Because Adam was a representative man, he would have brought himself and all his descendants into this rest if he had obeyed. But Adam sinned (and we sinned in him), so that pathway to Sabbath rest was closed to him (and us). The good news of the gospel is that the last Adam, Jesus Christ, has both obeyed where Adam disobeyed and paid the penalty for sins (1 Cor. 15), thereby securing Sabbath rest for human beings, who may only enter it through faith in him (Heb. 4).

Thus, the Old Testament is the account of God preparing the world for the appearing of his Son and the Son's accomplishment of redemption in his obedience, death, and resurrection. God does this by forming a people from Abraham. He redeems that people, Israel, from bondage in Egypt and then gives them his law. The Decalogue, which sits atop that law, includes the command to observe the Sabbath. The Sabbath reminds Israel not only of God's work of creation (Ex. 20) but also of his work of redemption (Deut. 5). God weaves the Sabbath into the warp and woof of the law that he gives his people through Moses: it is a sign of the Mosaic covenant, its transgression carries severe sanctions, it is the cornerstone of an extensive calendar for Israel's worship, and it points to Israel's ultimate failure to love and obey God.

Thus, after the Law, the Prophets highlight the Sabbath's violation as grounds for God's bringing covenant curses upon his disobedient people. Yet, the Sabbath is no less a vehicle for expressing the glorious and expansive restoration in Jesus Christ that God has in store for his people—God will accomplish his goal of drawing all kinds of human beings to himself in worship and fellowship. For this reason, the prophets' glorious vision of the future depicts all kinds of human beings observing and delighting in the Sabbath. And they show that God will do this work through a new shepherd-prince, a new covenant, and a new temple, all promises that look ahead to, converge upon, and find fulfillment in the person and finished work of the Lord Jesus Christ.

Overall, Jesus's earthly ministry took place largely under the Mosaic covenant. We see him regularly observing the Sabbath (and the other feasts and festivals required by the Mosaic law). We also see him showing the true meaning and purpose of the Sabbath. He teaches that the Sabbath points to the liberty and freedom from the condemnation, dominion, and curse of sin that he has come to secure for sinners (Luke 4). Further, his Sabbath miracles point to the rolling back of the curse and the restoration of human beings that his redemptive work will accomplish, and his healing of the man born blind shows the true purpose of the Sabbath—the worship of God in Christ (John 9). Last, his controversies with the Jewish leadership about the Sabbath offer a glimpse into his personal authority. Far from abrogating the Sabbath command, Jesus affirms it. As B. B. Warfield explains, "The Sabbath came out of Christ's hands . . . not despoiled of any of its authority or robbed of any of its glory, but rather enhanced in both authority and glory."[1] This happens when Jesus reaffirms its divinely intended meaning and purpose and removes all human accretions that had obscured and twisted that meaning and purpose—all on his own authority.

Thus, it is Jesus's divine and messianic authority that stamps his testimony to the Sabbath in Acts, the Letters, and Revelation. His resurrection on the first day of the week marks the dawn of the last days and the inbreaking of the new creation into human history. Because of this, the Sabbath undergoes corresponding transformation—

---

1. B. B. Warfield, "The Sabbath in the Word of God," in *Selected Shorter Writings*, ed. John E. Meeter, 2 vols. (Phillipsburg, NJ: P&R, 1971, 1973), 1:318.

God's people will observe the Sabbath on the first day of the week. Yet, the Sabbath continues to be a day of remembering God's finished work of creation and redemption, reminding the church of the rest that awaits them, the rest that Christ has secured for them by his life, death, and resurrection. As such, it is a day that the church, by the authority of the risen Christ, sets apart for the worship of God in Christ (Acts 20:7), and for this reason it takes on the name that it will bear until the end of the age—"the Lord's day" (Rev. 1:10).

The New Covenant Sabbath

What, then, does the observance of the Sabbath look like for people who live under the new covenant? We may begin to answer that question by reflecting upon the Sabbath along three lines—creation, Christ's work, and consummation.

CREATION

It is important to remember that the Sabbath's origin lies neither in the teaching of Jesus nor in the Mosaic commandments—it lies in the creation itself. As such, the Sabbath offers a critical, weekly reminder to human beings. Geerhardus Vos explains,

> There is to be to the world-process a finale, as there was an overture, and these two belong inseparably together . . . The Sabbath brings this principle of the eschatological structure of history to bear upon the mind of man after a symbolical and a typical fashion. It teaches its lesson through the rhythmical succession of six days of labor and one ensuing day of rest in each successive week. Man is reminded in this way that life is not an aimless existence, that a goal lies beyond.[2]

---

2. Geerhardus Vos, *Biblical Theology: Old and New Testaments* (Carlisle, PA: Banner of Truth, 1975), 140.

This dimension of the Sabbath is, perhaps, its most basic. God wants all people to remember that though human beings were made to work, he made them for more than work—he has made his image bearers for fellowship and communion with him. This worship is the goal of human existence and human history, and the Sabbath offers a weekly reminder of that goal. We exist in a world that often lives as though there was nothing beyond the five senses and as though momentary pleasures and satisfactions are the goal of life. In such a world, the Sabbath is a needed interruption and reality check. God made us so that he would be our "chiefest good," that "[he] and his glory" would be our "chiefest end."[3] Thus, the Sabbath provides a weekly reset to our priorities, attitudes, and goals so that we return to our callings of the other six days with the clarity and perspective that we need to live in a way that pleases and honors our great God.

CHRIST'S WORK

Part of how the Sabbath resets our lives is by pointing us to the work of Christ on our behalf. Under the Mosaic covenant, God called his people to look back upon their redemption from Egypt by his strong hand and mighty arm. The exodus, of course, shadowed the greater and final deliverance of God's people from sin through the death and resurrection of Jesus Christ (Luke 9:31; cf. 1 Pet. 2:9–10). Thus, on the Sabbath, we look back to what God has done in Jesus Christ to save sinners from the penalty, dominion, and power of sin. It is for this reason that God appointed the day of the Sabbath to be changed from the seventh day of the week to the first day of the week. On that first day, we remember that Christ was raised from the dead and that, because of this, sinners can be counted righteous through faith in Christ (Rom. 4:25; Acts 13:32–39). When a sinner is united

---

3. Thomas Goodwin, *The Works of Thomas Goodwin*, 12 vols. (Edinburgh: James Nichol, 1861-6), 6:459.

to Christ in his death and resurrection, he is no longer under the dominion of sin but now lives under the reign of grace (Rom. 6:1–14; 1 Pet. 1:3; 3:21).

What overwhelmingly characterizes Sabbath or Lord's Day observance in the New Testament is the people of God gathering to hear the word of God read and preached. And because, as Martin Luther once said, Christ is the center and circumference of the Scripture, to hear the word read and preached is to learn of the person and work of Jesus Christ (see Luke 24:25–27, 44–49). New covenant believers delight to remember what their Savior has done to bring them from condemnation to vindication, from the cruel bondage of sin to the service of Christ, whose "yoke is easy" and whose "burden is light" (Matt. 11:30). Thus, remembrance of Christ provides the standard for the gathered worship of Christians—sermons, prayers, psalms and hymns, baptism, and the Lord's Supper should all point people to Christ and him crucified, to Jesus Christ, risen from the dead (1 Cor. 2:2; 2 Tim. 2:8). And the fellowship of God's people—at all times, but especially on the Lord's Day—should find ways to encourage one another in and point one another toward the sufficiency and beauty of Christ as Savior from sin. Anything less trivializes their worship and fellowship and robs the day of the spiritual refreshment and joy that God intends for them to have through faith in Jesus Christ.

Consummation

Yet, the Sabbath not only points us back in time to the beginning and to the center of human history—it also points us ahead to the end of history. The author of the book of Hebrews reminds us that "there remains a Sabbath rest for the people of God" (Heb. 4:9). Here, the "rest" in view is the one that God held out to human beings at the creation (4:4), a rest that Adam—and we in Adam—failed to enter because of Adam's first sin. But the last Adam has secured that rest by his obedience, death, and resurrection; it is ours in Christ, even though it remains entirely future to us. Thus, the weekly Sabbath offers us regular reminders of the heavenly home that awaits us and that our earthly pilgrimage will one day come to a welcome conclusion.

This future orientation to the Sabbath has been in place since the creation. But, in Christ, this orientation takes on two added dimensions for the new covenant people of God. The first, as Vos observes, is that "the work which issues into the rest can no longer be man's own work. It becomes the work of Christ."[4] This principle was held "in common" in both the "Old Testament and the New Testament," with a critical "differ[ence]" of "perspective."[5] Vos continues,

> Inasmuch as the Old Covenant was still looking forward to the performance of the Messianic work, naturally the days of labour to it come first, the day of rest falls at the end of the week. We, under the New Covenant, look back upon the accomplished work of Christ. We, therefore, first celebrate the rest in principle procured by Christ, although the Sabbath also still remains a sign looking forward to the final eschatological rest.[6]

In other words, we are entirely dependent upon the finished work of Jesus Christ to enter the creation rest of God. In no way does anything that we have done, are doing, or shall do merit our entry into that rest. Part of our Sabbath celebration, then, is not only that Christ has delivered us from sin's penalty and dominion but that, in doing so, he has won for his people a secure place in the new

---

4. Vos, *Biblical Theology*, 141.
5. Vos, *Biblical Theology*, 141.
6. Vos, *Biblical Theology*, 141.

heavens and new earth. Thus, the Sabbath is a weekly reminder that we are entirely dependent upon Christ to bring us near to God. As we undertake the labors that God has appointed for us on the other six days, we remember that nothing that we will ever do in the work of our callings can supplement, much less replace, what Christ has done on our behalf.

Second, insofar as the weekly Sabbath points us forward to our future Sabbath rest, secured by Christ, we remember that we are a pilgrim people who have not yet arrived at our heavenly home. We are not, therefore, what we shall be, even as we are not yet where we shall one day be. This perspective, as Richard B. Gaffin Jr. reminds us, is a needed one in the Christian life. He explains,

> The weekly Sabbath is an important safeguard against the overreach "enthusiasm" that constantly threatens Christian faith; it protects the church against tendencies to blur or even lose sight of the differences between the eschatological "already" and "not yet." The Sabbath is a sure sign to the church that it is still "on the way," a recurring reminder to believers that while most assuredly they already belong to the new creation, are already resurrected with Christ, and daily are being renewed inwardly, still, in the body, in their psycho-physical existence, they are short of the final resurrection-rest that "awaits the people of God."[7]

This "enthusiasm" or triumphalism can take many forms— a crushing perfectionism that fails to reckon with the power and deception of indwelling sin in each believer; a quest for ecstatic or heightened spiritual experiences; a belief that good health and finan-

---

7. Richard B. Gaffin, Jr., "Westminster and the Sabbath," in ed. J. Ligon Duncan III, *The Westminster Confession into the 21st Century, Volume 1* (Fearn, Ross-shire, UK: Christian Focus, 2003), 139.

cial well-being are the norm for the faithful Christian; an expectation that the church I am part of should be free of sin and error. The Sabbath, insofar as it points us forward to the "not yet" of the Christian life, is a wholesome check against such distorted and destructive tendencies and impulses in the church today. And yet, the Sabbath does not do this in a way that robs us of gospel hope or consigns us to despair. There *is* a "not yet" and we *will* get there—in God's good time and in his good way.

Observing the Sabbath Today

In light of this summary of biblical teaching on the Sabbath, we may now take up some additional questions related to our practice of it. What does Sabbath observance look like in the twenty-first century? How do we honor the Lord's Day in a world that is committed to living for itself on a 24/7 basis? How does new covenant Sabbath observance look different from Israel's observance of the Sabbath? Thankfully, the church in the days of the apostles lived in a world similar to ours and reflected on the implications of Christ's finished work for the worship of God's people. As we bring this chapter to a close, we will explore three principles to hold to and three practical steps to take toward honoring this commandment that God has given to us for our good.

Three Principles

The first principle is that the Levitical calendar of the Old Testament—among the "shadows" pointing forward to Christ, the "substance" (Col. 2:16–17)—has answered its purpose in redemptive history. The elaborate system of feasts, festivals, and sacrifices prescribed by God in the Mosaic law has come to its appointed end with the resurrection of Christ from the dead. And to the degree that the weekly Sabbath participated in that shadowy anticipation, the Mosaic dimension of its observance has also come to an end.[8] Christ has consciously transformed the worship of God's people to reflect his finished work and the multinational character of the people of God (see John 4:21–24).

New covenant worship, then, is marked by simplicity. God's people gather in local assemblies one day a week. They hear the Bible read and preached, join their hearts in prayer, unite their voices in praise and thanksgiving, and observe baptism and the Lord's Supper according to Christ's commandment. It is through such simple and unassuming means, the New Testament tells us, that the Spirit is pleased to work in power both to draw people to Jesus Christ and to mature the church (see 1 Cor. 14:24–25; Eph. 4:11–16).

The second principle is that believers need to steer clear of the extremes of permissiveness on the one hand and of Pharisaism on the other hand.[9] The Lord's Day is not a time to pursue our own pleasures but what pleases God, as Isaiah reminds us (Isa. 58:13–14). The works that occupy Monday through Saturday will need to be consciously and deliberately set aside so that we will be free to devote the whole day to the worship of God. In this way we experience the rest that God intends for us—not the rest of selfishness and indolence, but the rest that leads us to our "deepest joy," namely, "the Lord" himself.[10]

Yet, Jesus also warns against a fundamentalism that robs the Sabbath of its joy by adding man-made commandments and prohibitions to what God has given us in his word. He was unsparing in his rebuke of the Jewish leadership for their dishonoring the authority of God and crushing the souls of God's people by turning a day of joy and rest into an unmitigated burden. Such an observance may appear devout and religious, but it is, in fact, an offense to God.

---

8. See further the helpful comments of Vos, *Biblical Theology*, 142–43.

9. J. Douma, *The Ten Commandments: Manual for the Christian Life*, trans. Nelson D. Kloosterman (Phillipsburg, NJ: P&R, 1996), 114–20.

10. Douma, *Ten Commandments*, 115.

Positively, then, what should this day look like for Christians? Jesus, the "lord of the Sabbath" (Matt. 12:8), points us to three kinds of works that are pleasing to him on his day. Preeminent is the work of public worship. Christ, by his own example and by the commands he gave through his apostles, tells us to sanctify the Lord's Day by coming together to worship our God and to enjoy the fellowship of God's people that comes alongside that worship. The second kind of work is what has been termed a work of necessity. Jesus, traveling with his disciples on the Sabbath, defended their plucking of grain to feed themselves. Similarly, preparing our meals, doing the dishes, and hanging up our church clothes are just a few modern examples of works of necessity. In addition to this, some professions properly require people to work every day and around the clock. Sickness, accidents, crime, and fires do not take Sundays off. For this reason, we need medical professionals, police officers, and firefighters to serve seven days a week. Christians involved in those professions may not want to volunteer their Sundays to work, but, if called to do so, they may work with a clear conscience. The third kind of work is what has been called a work of mercy. Jesus showed compassion to the sick and disabled by healing them, even on the Sabbath. In an analogous way, if, in God's providence, we encounter such needs in our lives on a Sunday, we should tend to those needs. If our young child is sick and needs to be watched, then we should stay home and care for her. If our pet is ill or hurt and needs to go to the vet, then we should take him to the vet to get the care that he needs.

The Bible does not give us a list of preapproved permitted and forbidden works on the Sabbath. Rather, God tells us that if we keep the main thing *the main thing* then the rest of the day should fall into place. If we set aside the work and entertainments that fill Monday through Saturday, if we prioritize public worship and fellowship with God's people, and if our hearts take sincere pleasure in communing with God, then we are in a good position to make God-honoring and biblical decisions about such details as these.

The third principle is that the Lord's Day offers tremendous benefit to God's people. Jesus reminds us that "the Sabbath was made for man, not man for the Sabbath" (Mark 2:27). God gave the Sabbath to help us, not to harm us. For one thing, the Sabbath is a help to our growth in grace as believers encourage one another in the pursuit of holiness (Heb. 10:24–25). Further, it reminds us of our certain and sure future Sabbath rest (Heb. 4:9) and gives us needed perspective in the face of trials and persecution (Rev. 1:10). The Sabbath is also a day when God's people tangibly express concern for one another through the taking up of a collection to relieve the needs of their brothers and sisters in Christ (1 Cor. 16:1–2). But above all, the Sabbath brings us near to Christ, who delights in drawing near to his gathered people to bless them through his word in the power of the Spirit. Thus, each Sabbath offers spiritual refreshment for parched and needy souls; a Sabbath well spent leaves us invigorated and ready to serve the Lord in the days ahead.

THREE PRACTICAL STEPS

So what are some practical steps that we can take to honor the Bible's teaching about the Sabbath? We may mention three in particular. The first is to set apart the whole day to God's worship. We should be members of a local church where the word is faithfully taught, and we should commit to attending services every week. Even if we are out of town, we should find a church where we may gather with fellow believers under the ministry of the word of God. If our church has an evening service, we should take advantage of that as well—to end the day as we began it, in the public worship of God. If our church does not have an evening service, we might pursue a Bible study in the afternoon or evening with other members of our church.

The second practical step is to find ways to enjoy Christian fellowship and extend hospitality on the Lord's Day. Invite fellow believers or visitors from your church to your home for a meal. Go to a local retirement home or nursing facility and visit church members who are unable to attend services. Call a believer who is lonely, discouraged, or weary and encourage them in the Lord. Take a walk with your spouse and share what you learned from the sermon that morning. If you have children, take advantage of the afternoon to go over what they learned in Sunday school and in church that morning. There are many ways to make good use of the Lord's Day in serving our fellow believers and our families. And, as always, when we serve others in ways that please God, we also find rich spiritual blessing in store for ourselves.

The third practical step is to seek spiritual refreshment on the Lord's Day. It would be tragic if the day were to devolve into a joyless succession of formal religious activity, much less a burden upon or interruption of pleasures sought and found elsewhere. God does want us to be engaged on his day, but the goal of our engagement is that we would know, more and more, the refreshment that comes from fellowship with our Maker and Redeemer.

In the Psalms, Asaph considered "the prosperity of the wicked" and confessed that his "feet had almost stumbled, [his] steps had nearly slipped" because of envy (Ps. 73:3, 2; see 73:4–15). He did not truly understand them or himself, he confesses, "until [he] went into the sanctuary of God" (Ps. 73:17). It was in the gathered worship of God (in the temple) that he understood two things. First, the pleasures of the wicked are illusory and transitory—"ruin" is what certainly lies in store for them (73:18). Second, the pleasures of the godly are real and certain. Asaph said to God,

> Nevertheless, I am continually with you;
>> you hold my right hand.

You guide me with your counsel,
    and afterward you will receive me to glory.
Whom have I in heaven but you?
    And there is nothing on earth that I desire besides you.
My flesh and my heart may fail,
    but God is the strength of my heart and my portion
        forever.
For behold, those who are far from you shall perish;
    you put an end to everyone who is unfaithful to you.
But for me it is good to be near God;
    I have made the Lord GOD my refuge,
    that I may tell of all your works. (Ps. 73:23–28)

Thus, Asaph badly needed a gospel reset to his perspective on the world and on himself, and God gave that to him when he entered the temple to worship. It was here that he was reminded of what he knew but had momentarily forgotten—God was leading him to glory; God was his chief desire; God would be with him until the end; the nearness of God was his good.

We need this reset more than we might like to admit. Our sinful thinking and the ungodliness of the world around us too often conspire to warp our perception of the way things really are. Thankfully, God provides us a gospel reset, and he does this every week. Like Asaph, we come to remember what we nearly forgot. We see our weakness and emptiness in light of God's strength and provision. We get a clear view of who God really is when we draw near to him. What could be more refreshing? Let us not only observe but enjoy the Sabbaths God gives us, until he brings us into that future and final Sabbath rest that Christ won for us, where "there is fullness of joy" and "pleasures forevermore" (Ps. 16:11).

General Index

Scripture Index

Short Studies in Biblical Theology Series

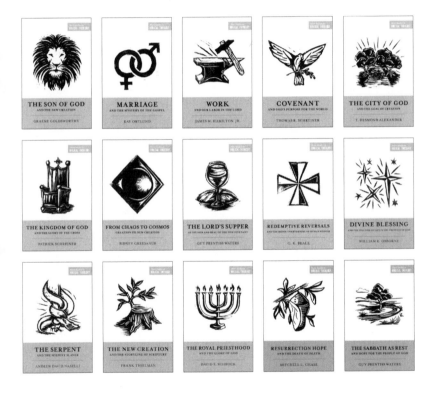

For more information, visit **crossway.org/ssbt**.